Law v. Order

LEGAL PROCESS AND FREE SPEECH
IN CONTEMPORARY FRANCE

Law v. Order

*Legal Process and Free Speech
in Contemporary France*

by

Jerome B. King

ARCHON BOOKS
1975

Library of Congress Cataloging in Publication Data

King, Jerome B.
    Law v. order.

    Bibliography: p.
    Includes index.
    1. Liberty of speech—France. I. Title.
Law   342′.44′085   75-8930
ISBN 0-208-01514-0

© 1975 by Jerome B. King
First published 1975 as an Archon Book,
an imprint of
The Shoe String Press, Inc.,
Hamden, Connecticut 06514

Printed in the United States of America

Contents

Preface

The law, the working of the law, the daily application of the law to people and situations, is an essential element in a country's life. It runs through everything: it is part of the pattern, like the architecture and the art and the look of the cultivated countryside. It shapes, and expresses, a country's mode of thought, its political concepts and realities, its conduct. It all hangs together whether the people themselves wish to acknowledge it or not, and the whole is a piece of the world we live in.

SYBILLE BEDFORD, *Faces of Justice*

This study aims to depict an inherently elusive subject—the spirit of a nation. The nation is France, and the aspect of her spirit I am after is civic spirit. Unfortunately for students of society, such subjects cannot be approached directly, for modern nations but rarely represent themselves in spiritual terms. And when they do, they do so in hypocritical disguises, as if they feared to lose their souls to some photographer's magic box, and had therefore to conceal the real meanings of their existence from profane and prying eyes. So if one is to come to grips at all with the "inarticulate major premises" of a country, he must do so by drawing inferences from the way its institutions work. This may be attempted in terms of political ideas, as Sybille Bedford suggests, and as I shall try to in this work. But how abstract ideas are specifically related to institutions, even legal ones, is seldom immediately apparent. Nor do those who experience these relationships as a matter of daily life ordinarily reflect, or have reason to reflect, on their general nature, for like old clothes, ideas lived in fit far more comfortably and naturally than ideas full of the starch of formal thought. To set forth relationships of ideas and institutions in such terms is to run certain risks of misrepresentation.

But where France is concerned, these risks seem worth taking because the French themselves—and not least by their own accounts—are notorious for their *incivisme*, or lack of civic spirit. This is to say that France has long appeared to pose an essential problem as much to herself as to political science. It is a problem easily stated: how do citizens with so little apparent civic spirit manage to constitute a nation at all? What is there in this place called France and this history called French to hold together people so seemingly committed to mutual suspicions of one another's opinions and behavior that they incline to view even democratic government as an occupying power, tax collectors and other agents of the State as public enemies, and the Republic itself as little more than bureaucratic inertia?

The question suggests what civic spirit is, and what role it plays. It infuses the community with solidarity, and thereby reflects the community's sense that its collective destiny is in some measure in its own hands. From Aristotle's *koinonia* to Marx's class consciousness, virtually every political thinker of the Western world has emphasized in one way or another the importance of the bonds which hold political groups together. Even classical liberals, who generally assumed a sort of atomic individualism, usually resort to at least one shared understanding, such as mutual forbearance. "Do not do unto others as you would not have them do unto you" constitutes a sort of leitmotiv to Thomas Hobbes's *Leviathan*, for example. And Adam Smith argued an unseen hand projecting the public good from private competition of all engaged in according to self-interest.[1]

Civic spirit is therefore a certain mind set that runs through all of political life. It is a force for inclusion and exclusion. It identifies groups to themselves and members of the group to one another. And by the same token it indicates those who do not belong, those who are outsiders, because they do not share the same outlook. Civic spirit nourishes community, in short, and one way it accomplishes its essential task is to activate the mechanisms of immunity against ideas which threaten cohesiveness. Hence civic spirit involves a principle of censorship, and so serves in every nation of the world.

This assertion may seem perverse to some contemporary liberals, though perhaps less so than it would have a generation ago. Then it was widely believed in our so-called "free world" that nations fell either into the category of those that maintained a "free marketplace of ideas" or into one in which politics was "ideological" and thus of an inherently totalitarian character. But it is now more generally recognized that the notion of a "free marketplace of ideas" pushes factors making for censorship back to a subconscious stage, making them both more effective and less vulnerable to self-conscious analysis.

Tocqueville was perhaps the first to make this point, at least so far as the United States was concerned, in his celebrated observations about the "tyranny of the majority." This tyranny was not an institutional matter, nor simply a consequence of accepting the principle of majority vote. It was, rather, an essential characteristic of the American outlook. Hence his comment that he knew of "no country in which there is generally so little independence of mind and real freedom of discussion as in America."[2] What he meant was that we were a nation of people for whom political and economic activities did not give rise to new moral perspectives:

> In the moral world, everything is classified, systematized, foreseen, and decided beforehand; in the political world, everything is agitated, disputed, and uncertain. In the one is a passive though voluntary obedience; in the other an independence scornful of experience, and jealous of all authority. These two tendencies, apparently so discrepant, are far from conflicting; they advance together, and mutually support each other. Religion perceives that civil liberty affords a noble exercise to the faculties of man, and that the political field is prepared by the Creator for the efforts of the mind. Free and powerful in its own sphere . . . religion

never more surely establishes its empire than when it reigns in the hearts of men unsupported by aught besides its native strength.

Liberty regards religion as its companion in all its battles and triumphs—as the cradle of its infancy, and the divine source of its claims. It considers religion as the safeguard of morality, and morality as the best security of the law, and [thus] the surest pledge for the duration of freedom. . . .[3]

In brief, the civic spirit animating our political liberties depended ultimately on a fixed and unquestioned moral horizon shared virtually by all Americans alike. If freedom of speech and conscience, and freedom of thought, were among "God's greatest gifts to Americans," as Mark Twain once commented, it was just because they were accompanied by a still greater gift—the "prudence never to practice either." We Americans have, in short, forestalled a great deal of governmental or public censorship by censoring ourselves. We have been "responsible" members of the community because our shared expectations about political life have seldom risen above a measure of satisfaction of our economic needs as these have been conventionally defined. And by restricting ourselves to making only such claims, by our willingness to treat ideas as if they were merely goods and services to be bought and sold for private advantage in the "free marketplace," we have, and not in the least paradoxically, each done our bit to support the moral and mental framework within which such claims are treated as the only suitable stuff of politics. It is thus that most political struggles in America, far from weakening our civic spirit, have tended to reinforce it. The more conflicts of "enlightened self-interest" we have engaged in, the more deeply have we felt ourselves to be one people sharing the same approach to a common destiny. Conversely, when our conflicts have been phrased in terms of national purpose or goal, the more we have been frustrated and divided by them.

Now for all the frustrations and divisions of her public life France is indubitably a nation. There must therefore be some kind of a mind set that may be said to be characteristically

French. The fact that she has a great deal more experience than we Americans have had with the legal control of free speech, and with public censorship, suggests, however, that whatever this mind set may be, it is hardly identical with the civic spirit of America. On the other hand, it is certain that many French people do regard their own fellow citizens as lacking in civic spirit. Hence though the ideal of the "responsible citizen" doing his share to maintain and uphold the common patrimony is certainly not wholly congruent with the practice of citizenship in France, it cannot simply be ignored either. Indeed, the notion of personal responsibility—of what is responsible behavior—is a key to the question here, all the more so because it has its formal counterpart in the idea of legal liability. By identifying those who are specifically liable for specific acts in specific situations the law and the courts reflect an authoritative view of social order.

I say "the law and the courts" because statutes are merely general and abstract. Taken by themselves they cannot tell us how the law really works. It is in their application alone that legal rules take on concrete social meaning. It is in the work of the courts—their procedures, their understandings, and their rulings—that we are likely to find an especially good clue to a sense of the community itself.

This is so because the courts are naturally engaged in what is ultimately a metaphysical business: they relate words to things and vice versa, so that both may assume a meaning on which authoritative and persuasive judgments may be based. This character of legal operations is nowhere better illustrated than in judicial attempts to regulate speech and press, for in this field the *corpus delicti* rests peculiarly on the interpretation of the circumstances. Homicide is homicide wherever you find it, and whatever the varying kinds of legal names—murder, manslaughter, involuntary or not—which may later be applied to it. This is to say that with homicide we begin with the notion that a violent death is wrong in and of itself, whatever its causes, and it strikes us as right that public authorities should determine what led to this wrong, and who was responsible.

The case of speech acts is, on the other hand, somewhat

different. A presumption of injury or wrong does not necessarily lie with the very words used in a particular speech act, as it can with a physical act of violence. In a libertarian society, indeed, there are good reasons for presuming speech acts of many kinds to be at least harmless if not actually useful, so that our legal procedures demand some particular circumstances which would justify their author's being accused and tried, to say nothing of being found guilty.[4] This presumption of harmlessness for words has been expressed in American law by Justice Holmes, who wrote in a famous opinion that

> The question in every case is whether the words used are used in such circumstances and are of such a nature as to create a clear and present danger that they will bring about the substantive evils that Congress has a right to prevent. It is a question of proximity and degree.[5]

This same presumption of innocence approach found expression four decades earlier during the debates of the French parliament, concerning the bill that was to become the Press Law of 1881, legislation that is still the basic statute regulating free speech in France today. It was a presumption reflecting much nineteenth-century experience, for before 1881 French authors had felt the weight of laws punishing so-called *délits d'opinion*. These were offenses whose definition did not require reference to matters of "proximity and degree" but simply to a comparison of two texts, that of the law on the one hand and that of the "speech act" on the other. In the generally liberal and libertarian push of the Third Republic's beginnings, this feature of the legal tradition was considered particularly odious, and the debates of 1881 make it clear that the intent of the legislators was to do away with *délits d'opinion* altogether. One of the devices they fastened on to accomplish their purpose was to bring the jury into a far wider range of cases than had been considered acceptable under the IInd Empire, on the premise that only a jury could represent the public's sense of the "proximity and degree" adequately. Like Holmes, in short, the French legislators wanted to create a law the practical application of which would depend on the relationship between the circumstances and the "nature" of the words spoken or published, rather than simply on their putative nature alone.

For the French libertarians of the 1880s, then, no idea was to be forbidden expression simply because of its allegedly harmful character. Legal control was to be brought into play only to redress an identifiable wrong in some particular, concrete social context. And only a jury drawn from that context was thought to have an authoritative view of whether such a wrong had in fact been committed.

As we shall presently see, French law, particularly with respect to the role of juries, is very different today. But a key element of it necessarily remains, and that is the factor of knowledge *(scienter)*. This is to say that the mechanisms determining legal liability inevitably depend on court-instituted processes of discovery of the state of mind of the defendant, on the ground that legal liability can exist only when the agent's malice or negligence is proved. For fundamental to the whole notion of personal responsibility in law is that the norms of the community must in some measure be reflected in the agent's own awareness of the act of which he stands accused. If this condition is not met, the law itself becomes irrelevant, because the defendant and the public never meet, mentally or morally speaking, at all.[6]

The method of my work is therefore to show how the French legal system today discovers the kind of knowledge necessary to assign legal liability, in order to suggest how these processes reveal characteristics of French civic spirit.

The most obvious feature of these processes appears immediately in the duality of French courts—administrative, on the one hand, and ordinary (criminal and civil), on the other. In matters of free speech the very existence of a distinct and well-developed system of administrative law, with its own set of courts and judges, has meant that the legal liability of public officials responsible for maintenance of public order against potential disturbances caused by speech acts is defined in ways different from those employed by the ordinary courts to define and attribute liability to private speakers or authors. This formal division of laws and courts with respect to speech and press is indeed all the more striking because it has been a wholly customary development in French legal history, apparently corresponding to a deeper and more constant imperative of the culture than any of those conscious efforts to rewrite the formal constitution which have marked her political life from 1871 to the present day. As I shall show later, this imperative appears to express itself in legal practice regarding free speech in these terms: the policing of public order in its physical aspects is primarily the responsibility of public officials; the private citizen is responsible for self-policing only in the realm of moral order.

This study will, therefore, first point to certain distinctions between the administrative and ordinary jurisdiction, their respective forms of action, and the methods of reasoning that mark their different operation in the realm of free speech. By illustrating ways in which determination and knowledge of the circumstances surrounding the dissemination of ideas and opinions have been used by French courts to determine the guilt or innocence of private citizens on the one hand, and the legality of censorship or prior restraint by public officials on the other, I mean to draw attention to the potential for conflict between the respective processes of the two court systems, in order to draw therefrom inferences about how the highly formalized perspectives of the legal system reflect and reinforce general views about the compound nature of political life.

From this analysis I am led to conclude how the distinctions between private and public law, as they are worked out in France, correspond to a profound sense of how difficult it is in the French tradition to equate law with order, or even to take law and order as being naturally joined by the conjunction *and*. Attempts of her legal system to distinguish and at the same time reconcile the work of two jurisdictions reveal a profound tension lying at the heart of the French constitution. This tension is to be found, in short, not just in the legal system but in the French view of politics to such a degree that it typifies civic spirit itself.

But surely, you may argue, the tension described here between law and order in France reflects at most a difference of degree with American views. Are we not aware that laws defining civil liberties must be outweighed by considerations of expedience in moments of crisis? What else are many of the leading cases in American constitutional law concerning free speech than commentaries upon this balance?

It is my contention, however, that in this difference of degree —if that is all it is—lies an essential difference between the spirit of French and American legal and political life. What is to us an exception to the normal course of events, and an exception, furthermore, which falls within our broad assumption that the moral order of society is really indistinguishable from its physical order, is in France a matter recognized by the basic structures and modes of the legal system. There the tension between law and order is built into every succeeding generation not only by the alarums and excursions of history but by the legal tradition itself.

The emphasis on the uniqueness of the French outlook in this work raises the question as to whether the peculiarities of other cultures are of more interest to us than their similarities. Certain canons of contemporary social science are sometimes said to impose a requirement of searching for universal laws of human behavior, the very word *law* in this context connoting universality. Without entering the argument about whether the behavior of social man is not rather better understood in terms of his capacity to make and apply rules than in terms of an unconscious reflection of scientific laws, I can only respond by saying that I think it a mistake to demand the imposition of one exclusive form of logic on anything as multiform and human institutions and activities. "There are more things in heaven and earth, Horatio, than are dreamt of in your philosophy," and I cannot see how it does much good to say that social analyses which fail to fit operationally logical patterns are somehow less real or important than those that appear to.

This said, however, it is clear that the work here does employ a classification or typology of political culture taken in one of its aspects, and that the more serious charge against it must come from those who doubt whether patterns of human institutions, even legal ones, are of as broad significance as I attempt to paint them here, or that my description is either characteristic or uniquely appropriate to France. To such charges as these I can only reply in the words of Thomas Hobbes:

> But let one man read another by his actions never so perfectly, it serves him only with his acquaintance, which are but few. He that is to [know] a whole nation must read in himself, not this or that particular man, but mankind; which though it be hard to do, harder than to learn any language or science, yet when I have set down my own reading orderly and perspicuously the pains left another will be only to consider if he also find not the same in himself. For this kind of doctrine admits no other demonstration.[7]

There will also be those skeptical about whether it is possible to interpret specific legal practices, as I have tried to do here, in the light of political ideas. Prudent men have wandered lifetimes in the mazes of the law, after all, and been more loathe to generalize about it at the end of their explorations than they were at the beginning. Without gainsaying scruples of legal scholarship, I should remind my readers that if there is in some measure a common language for law and politics that language is one of morals. I have therefore tried to present the materials of this study in the light of ethical considerations, even where these have not been explicit. And this attempt has been made not only that some sense could be made of legal practices in political terms, but also so that the work should make allowance for a principle of John Stuart Mill that seems to me a good one to keep in mind for comparative studies in general:

> The true teacher of the fitting social arrangements for England, France, or America, is the one who can point out how the English, French, or American character can be improved, and how it has been made what it is. A philosophy of laws and institutions, not founded on a philosophy of national character, is an absurdity.[8]

16

Though not aspiring directly here to the improvement of any nation's character, nor hoping to avoid all absurdities, I do believe that considerations of the kind raised in this study are ones political teaching must reckon with, and perhaps to be of special interest to Americans at a time when their own values appear increasingly to be in question.

Acknowledgements

This study was originally funded by a Ford Public Affairs Grant administered by the Williams College Public Affairs Committee. Research in France was facilitated by two members of the Bar of Aix-en-Provence, Maître Yves Michelot and Maître Max Juvenal, and Professor Gérard Marcy of the Law Faculty of the University of Aix-Marseille. A year at Harvard Law School under the auspices of a Carnegie Fellowship in Law later made available the time and the perfect environment for thinking through the research materials.

Professors Harold Berman, and Arthur von Mehren of Harvard Law School, Henry Ehrmann of Dartmouth College, James Burns, Robert Gaudino, Francis Oakley, and Daniel O'Connor of Williams College, Dwight Simpson of San Francisco State, Loren Beth of the University of Massachusetts, and Laurence Wylie of Harvard University have all provided valuable suggestions on various drafts, and invaluable encouragement. The great obligation I am under to each of them, and to my own family in three generations, of course implies no responsibility on their part for the shortcomings of this work.

J. B. K.

Law v. Order

LEGAL PROCESS AND FREE SPEECH
IN CONTEMPORARY FRANCE

CHAPTER ONE

The Conflict
between Law and Order

It is my wish to inquire whether it is possible . . . to discover a legitimate and stable basis of government . .. . I shall attempt to maintain a constant connection between what right permits and interest demands, so that no separation may be made between justice and utility.

J. J. Rousseau, *The Social Contract*

Happy are those people for whom justice blooms on the rude stem of utility. Since a broad sense of expedience nourishes their sense of both law and order with the same food, only the greatest of catastrophes can shake their constitutions. Circumstances less than collectively fatal but serve as additional evidence of successful adaptation to the forces of history. Such peoples take it for granted that they have a "constitution intended to endure for ages to come," as Chief Justice John Marshall once wrote for his fellow Americans in 1819, "and, consequently, to be adapted to the various *crises* of human affairs."[1]

The French are not an altogether happy people. Far from it, indeed. Their modern constitution, in the broadest sense of the term, reflects in its structures and processes a sharp awareness that the need for order in the face of "the various crises of human affairs" and the demand for justice by no means tend spontaneously in the same direction, or are even to be rendered wholly compatible by human institutions. From this awareness arises a persistent rejection of the very idea of spontaneous

21

and incremental constitutional development, a rejection that is accompanied by a search for justice in formal ideas rather than in the stuff of history. And yet not without reservations. For though the ideas of liberty, equality, and fraternity have for many years now been customarily celebrated in public ceremony, we need hardly attend carefully to French political rites to hear an accompanying liturgy directed toward the idols of family, private property, and the forces of order.

Contemporary France suffers, in short, from a certain split personality. The tensions of this split are no doubt reflected in many ways. But they are perhaps nowhere more clearly institutionalized than in her legal system, with its dual jurisdictions, each dealing in its respective ways with freedom of speech. The different and sometimes even contradictory modes in which this basic constitutional liberty is defined by the administrative courts on the one hand, and by the ordinary criminal and civil courts on the other, suggest that at least for Frenchmen in this century justice is born only in cruel labor and maintained only by a high pitch of consciousness of the ironies of human life.

This state of mind does not make the French a particularly easy people to live with, least of all for themselves. But it may well place them among the most modern peoples on earth. For in this day and age, when the pursuit of social utility is beginning to appear as uncertain and even as dangerous as the search for justice has often proved, who is to say that man's freedom will not be as well served by an ironic view of history as by one which takes political stability through constitutional evolution as evidence of divine grace?

But such a question lies beyond this study, which focuses on legal processes and should thus begin with a legal drama. The circumstances of this story arose, symbolically perhaps, near the geographical heart of France in the small city of Nevers during the winter of 1930. There and then occurred a series of events which eventually led to a notable legal case concerning freedom of speech.[2] It is notable because it illustrates one of the fundamental preoccupations of the French legal system—to maintain that "constant connection between what right permits and interest demands" which Rousseau sought, and thus to reconcile law with order. In so doing, the story opens the way to an understanding of how the very structure of the legal system at once reflects and helps maintain French "unhappiness," and how this unhappiness appears in political life as the familiar extremes of *incivisme* and revolutionary *élan*. And it is to an understanding of this Janus-like spirit that this study is devoted.

On the morning of February 19, 1930, the Mayor of Nevers found a strongly worded letter on his desk. He certainly already knew what the letter was about. Should he have been tempted to ignore it, however, its authors had made a point of having it published the same day in *La Tribune du Centre*, the local newspaper of Socialist sympathies.

February 18, 1930

Monsieur le maire;

We have the honor to bring to your attention the following resolution, unanimously adopted by the Executive Council of the Nièvre branch of the National Syndicate of Public Elementary School Teachers . . . during its session of February 6:

The Council is informed that a lecture by M. René Benjamin has been scheduled on the program of the *Galas littéraires*.[3] The Council is astounded that the *syndicat d'initiative*,[4] which surely ought to conduct its activities in a neutral manner, should have chosen an enthusiastic supporter of *Action française*,[5] and is above all struck to note that the invitation has been made to the very person who has gained notoriety during the past few years by acts which have caused violent protests everywhere (Dôle, Epinal, Loches, Bordeaux, Poitiers, St. Etienne, etc.). In a book which is nothing but a tissue of invectives, and in even more ignominious newspaper articles, he has indulged himself in vulgar attacks upon public school teaching personnel, on the quality of the instruction given, and on the students formed thereby. It is no longer a matter of polemics, which are always legitimate so long as they take the form of an exchange of views, but of defamatory attacks which demand an answer. René Benjamin has thrown down a challenge to public school teachers which they, however little they may care to do so, are under obligation to take up. To this end the Council has decided to organize a demonstration, scheduled for the same day as the lecture, which will show René Benjamin and his friends the real feelings of the teachers and supporters of public education in the Nièvre. And it is asking all workers and all political groups on the Left kindly to associate themselves with this demonstration.

Most respectfully,

[signed]

Upon receipt of this letter, the Mayor turned to the Prefect of the Nièvre, whose seat was Nevers, for advice. This representative of France's central government advised him that all mayors had the duty, under provisions of the Law on Municipal Organization of April 5, 1884, to maintain order in their communes. But how? Should the Mayor forbid Benjamin to speak? Or should he hope to maintain order by calling out the police? This was the critical question and, to the Mayor's chagrin, it was one on which the Prefect did not express any opinion.

Two and one-half weeks before Benjamin's first scheduled appearance on March 11, the protest campaign became increasingly active. Tracts now littered the streets and posters were put up on every available wall, often to be defaced by passersby of opposing views. *La Tribune du Centre*, having published the teachers' open letter to the Mayor, became a major means of communication for those who opposed Benjamin's appearance, printing both "eye-witness" reports of the disturbances which his visits had allegedly touched off elsewhere, and a schedule of the planned demonstration for the benefit of "all political groups on the Left."

On February 25 the Mayor came to his first decision. Listing the towns where Benjamin's talks had apparently caused trouble before, and noting those provisions of the Law of April 5, 1884, which gave mayors responsibility for maintaining order, this decision took the form of an official decree that concluded:

Whereas the information presented allows us to consider

the impending visit of M. René Benjamin to be of such a nature as to disturb public order, and whereas it is most important to spare the people the spectacle of regrettable incidents; [The Mayor] Decrees:

Article I—The public lecture listed in the program of the *Galas littéraires* and organized by the *syndicat d'initiative* is prohibited at the *Ciné-Parc* and all other public places.

The wording of this decree no doubt suggested to Benjamin's supporters their next tactic. A brief advertisement appeared shortly in the local newspapers calling attention to the substitution of a "private" meeting for the prohibitcd public one. Although date and place remained the same, tickets were now to be required. They could be obtained, the advertisement said, at the box office of the *Ciné-Parc* at any time. And they were to be free.

The Mayor's response to this announcement came the very day of Benjamin's first scheduled appearance. It was another ban. Noting that there appeared to be no difference between the private and public meeting in this instance, the Mayor found it "important to avoid every kind of provocation and demonstration" because, he said, "political groups appear desirous of taking advantage of the occasion to disturb order in the streets." Having seen to the posting of this second decree, he himself then proceeded to lead a demonstration "of all workers and all political groups on the Left" to the city's principal marketplace, which the Socialists had reserved in advance for this very purpose.

Mr. Benjamin showed somewhat more discretion. Giving up his talk as ordered, he appealed to the law against the Mayor's decrees. In following this course, he came to enjoy the support of Nevers' *syndicat d'initiative* and the nationwide *Société des gens de lettres*, the latter asking to be co-plaintiff with Benjamin.

In due course, the case came before the litigation branch (*section du contentieux*) of the Council of State (*Conseil d'Etat*) in Paris, France's highest administrative court. Decision was handed down on May 19, 1933—three years, two months, and eight days after the date when Benjamin's appearance in Nevers was to have endangered the tranquillity of her gray walls and cobblestoned streets.

The Council's decision read as follows:

The Council of State:—

Having in view the Laws of June 30, 1881 and March 27, 1907, the Law of April 5, 1884, the Laws of October 7-14, 1780 and May 24, 1872 decides:

On the standing of the Literary Society: Considering that the Society . . . has an interest in the annulment of [the Mayor's] decisions here challenged . . . , its standing in this lawsuit is valid;

On the legality of the [Mayor's] decisions here challenged: Considering that though it is incumbent upon a mayor, by virtue of Article 97 of the Law of April 5, 1884, to take all measures necessary to maintain public order, he must nevertheless reconcile exercise of his powers with the freedom of meeting guaranteed by the Laws of June 30, 1881 and March 29, 1907; and,

Considering that in order to forbid the lectures of M. Benjamin listed in the program of the *Galas littéraires* organized by the *syndicat d'initiative* of the City of Nevers, both of which had the character of public meetings, the Mayor argued that M. Benjamin's visit to Nevers was of a kind to disturb public order; and considering that [our] inquiry shows the possibility of disorder, as asserted by the Mayor . . . not to have presented such a degree of gravity as to have rendered impossible the maintenance of order by other police measures than the one actually taken of prohibiting the lectures; and that as a consequence, without its being necessary to decide on plaintiffs' plea concerning malfeasance in office (*détournement de pouvoir*), plaintiffs are justified in maintaining that the Mayor's . . . decisions were beyond his rightful powers (*entachés d'exces de pouvoir*), and hence void;

Decrees:

Article I: The standing of the Literary Society is upheld;
Article II: The decisions of the Mayor of Nevers are annulled.

As novices in the art of interpreting French judicial decisions, we are struck by the dryness of this opinion. It vindicated Benjamin's claim to speak and declared void the Mayor's prohibition. What more can be said?

We note immediately that the issue of prior restraint was central. When an official fears for the public order and says "no" to a speaker, what form of censorship can be more complete, what derogation of the principle of free speech apparently more thoroughgoing? So far as Angle-American jurisprudence is concerned, this kind of control was ostensibly abandoned during the course of the eighteenth century. We have it on Blackstone's authority, for example, that

> The *liberty of the press* is indeed essential to the nature of a free state; but this consists in laying no previous restraints upon publications, and not in freedom from censure for criminal matters when published. Every freeman has an undoubted right to say what sentiments he pleases before the public: to forbid this is to destroy the freedom of the press: but if he publishes what is improper, mischievous, or illegal, he must take the consequences of his own temerity. . . . Thus, the will of individuals is still left free; the abuse only of that freewill is the object of legal punishment. . . .[6]

We should therefore suppose that when a case analogous to Benjamin's arises in the United States or England, the speaker's right would be vindicated without reserve. The wording of the Article II of the French Declaration of the Rights of Man (1789) may indeed incline us to suppose that the same general state of affairs must also be characteristic of French law because it asserts that:

27

Every citizen may henceforward speak, write, and publish freely, except to answer for the abuse of this liberty in those cases determined by law.

Yet there is nothing in the Council's decision to suggest that the Mayor of Nevers acted without a shadow of legal backing. Far from denying his police powers, the Council of State declared only that he had used the wrong kind in the instant case. We are left with the implication that under a clearer and more present danger the Mayor's decree would have been found lawful.

Furthermore, annullment of the Mayor's acts of prior restraint must have given plaintiff Benjamin little more than moral satisfaction, and perhaps not even much of that. For though the Mayor may have been legally ill-advised in his ban, it certainly had effect on the only date—March 11, 1930—when it would have done Benjamin much good to have its illegality declared.

Indeed, the mills of justice not only ground at their usual stately pace, they also ground out finer distinctions that Benjamin had been seeking. For the decision mentions in passing that plaintiff was asking for a harsher judgment against the Mayor than the court was willing to give. The issue could be decided, it said, without reference to the argument alleging malfeasance in office. The plaintiff doubtless had in mind the Mayor's proclaiming the necessity of avoiding "all provocations and demonstrations" while preparing personally to lead a demonstration to satisfy, in the words of the Council of State's *commissaire du gouvernement*, his "political friends." Had Benjamin been successful in this specific plea, it could have opened the possibility of collecting damages from the Mayor personally, thus providing *Action française* with more good publicity.[7] But the judges of the Council of State refused to open that door. So the Mayor's wrongness does not seem to have taken a very grave form in their eyes. He probably continued on in office much as before, more concerned about the opinions of his constituents in Nevers than of some administrative mandarins in Paris.

Whatever the constitutional aspects of the matter, furthermore, we don't have to read very much between the lines to guess that the Mayor's decision to ban Benjamin's lectures was owing more to his fear of the political consequences of protecting Benjamin's right to appear than fear of public disorder. The right wing reactionary movement *Action française* was then approaching new prominence in its course through the Third Republic's checkered history, and Nevers' *syndicat d'initiative* could hardly have invited Benjamin in ignorance of his relationship to that movement or of its political views. Even the title of his talks gave a clue, for whatever their merits as literary figures, Courteline and Guitry were well known for their mordant attacks on republicanism and the parliamentary system. In fact, Guitry was many years later to be sentenced by a Liberation court—some think wrongly—for collaboration with the Germans. The allegation that Benjamin's appearance had disturbed the peace in other places, in any case, was hardly disputed. Didn't Nevers, as *La Tribune du Centre* put it, have the duty to prevent its hospitality from being abused by "outsiders" like Benjamin, who came "to sow hatred and discord" within "our fair city"? The city's problem was not so much Benjamin's sowing hatred, however, as his harvesting it. Surely the Mayor was aware that his political supporters would hardly forgive him for allowing their city to provide a protected platform for an important representative of political ideas they particularly loathed.

What at first is more difficult to understand is why Benjamin was satisfied to pursue his cause through the legal system. *Action française* was hardly a friend of the rule of law nor of the Third Republic. And the previous disorders suggest few scruples on Benjamin's part about provoking them. Since Nevers was apparently ripe for trouble why did he not, by ignoring the Mayor's ban, go on to provoke a disturbance there, too? Arrest could well have been the first result. But arrest at the hands of a Socialist mayor could only have given more flavor to the *Action française's* bitterly anti-Republican potion.

A remark in the presentation of the case before the Council of State by the *commissaire du gouvernement* provides material for speculation here.[8] In recommending to his colleagues that the Mayor's ban be annulled, he reported that Benjamin's talk was to have been of a purely "literary" nature. Now surely *Commissaire* Michel could not have made this assertion without some reflection. It suggests the possibility that Benjamin had brought his cause to the bar because he was hoping to elicit from the Council of State a reflection of its political, not literary or legal, views. Councillors of State were then generally reputed to be sympathetic to the political Right. Its judges were recruited largely from the Parisian upper bourgeoisie, and from what other group would reactionaries then be more likely drawn.?[9] If his case could show the Council of State to be openly in tune with the political sentiments of the *Action française*, Benjamin probably thought his forbearance at Nevers would be amply compensated.

If this was his hope, it reveals a misjudgment of the distinction between law and order essential to an appreciation of French constitutionalism. Right turned out to be on Benjamin's side, of course, but more in a poetic than practical sense. For though it did remind a fiercely republican mayor that the exercise of administrative duties was limited by law, the Council of State vindicated only abstractly the legally guaranteed right of free speech. Right ultimately had its day in court. But of State vindicated only abstractly the legally guaranteed right of free speech. Right ultimately had its day in court. But order had its way on the streets.

Now if a person may in fact be prevented from speaking because some official fears that expression of his views constitute a clear and immediate danger to public order, how far are contemporary Frenchmen from the situation complained of by Beaumarchais' Figaro?

> Provided that my writings mention neither authority nor religion, neither politics nor morals, nor people of standing nor those in favor, not the Opera nor any other spectacles, nor any person who associates himself with anything, I can freely publish under the eyes of only two or three censors.[10]

Despite immediate appearances to the contrary, I think they are very far indeed. For however honored in legal thought

Blackstone's distinction between prior restraint and ex post facto punishment be, it does divert attention from one aspect of the question very deserving of it. For what is the meaning of the threat of criminal sanctions if not to deter? Where the threat of criminal sanctions is aimed at deterring the expression of ideas, its intention and potential effect can be just as much prior censorship as that which may be exercised externally by a public official. This is to say that whatever the public interest in retribution against him who speaks "improper, mischievous, and illegal" views, it is far less than in simple prevention of their propagation. To leave the choice of censoring himself or not to the individual's own choice sounds libertarian in principle. But it quite overlooks the possibility that self-censorship must operate at a deeper and broader level than that of fear of the policeman or the mob. To be effective as a support of the social order, it must operate on habits of thinking themselves. In this way not only is speech censored; so also are the activities of mind which nourish speech.[11]

We must therefore ask whether Blackstone's distinction between censorship and punishment is as appropriate to analysis of the real constitution of a regime as would be a distinction between censorship exercised by a public official and censorship exercised by the habits of thought of the private person's mind. Since this latter distinction is emphasized by the operations of the French legal system, we shall look at certain of its implications, both in practical terms and in those which reflect the spirit of French constitutionalism. Let us do so by turning again to the Benjamin case.

Is it not perhaps misleading to say that the only moral of this case is that right may have its day in court so long as order has its way on the streets? Do not both law and order ultimately depend on the same symbols? The Council of State certainly implied its own belief that this is true by calling for a "reconciliation" between the exercise of fundamental liberties and the exercise of police powers, between "what right permits" and "interest demands"?

Take first what "right permits." Here, the standing which the Council of State gave to the *Société des gens de lettres* provides a clue. This Society is a private voluntary association recognized in French law as being of a *utilité publique*, which is to say a group representing a moral cause that has certain legal rights, recognized by statute. The group asked to appear in court on Benjamin's behalf in order "to defend, in the strictly literary realm, the freedom of the speaker and writer, whoever he may be." The scope of this claim is worthy of note. While obviously far broader than the defense of what was undoubtedly a contract between Benjamin and Nevers' *syndicat d'initiative*, it nevertheless asked for freedom only in the "strictly literary realm." And if we may judge from the *commissaire du gouvernement's* statement of the case, the judges took the position offered by the Literary Society. This is to say, Benjamin's cause was argued and probably won on the basis of distinction between its literary and political merits.

In the light of the trouble he had apparently enjoyed provoking at other times and places, this distinction must have been frustrating to Benjamin himself. *Action française*, of which he was then a major spokesman, had certainly never shown any disposition to consider literature and politics to be distinct enterprises, nor the latter subordinate to the former. Nor were the public school teachers protesting Benjamin's appearance in Nevers in any doubt about his political intentions. But Benjamin's lawyers undoubtedly knew what arguments the Council would receive best, and so a claim based on "the strictly literary realm" was proposed. Such a limitation surely made it easier for the Council to see where the line between right and expediency would fall. For however great the French literary effervescence, the judges must have thought conflicts between public order and letters less touchy than those between order and politics.

Yet even more important was the character thus assigned to Benjamin's claim. For what is the "strictly literary realm"? Plaintiffs' lawyers probably meant to suggest that Benjamin's political ideas were only incidental to his literary ones and thus not to be weighed in the balancing of interests to take place.

But if this inference is drawn, it means that Benjamin's right was not derived from his function as a citizen; he was not asking a right on behalf of the public as represented in the audience he should have had that March evening in Nevers to participate in political processes. He was rather speaking only as an individual developing his own personality by means of the "most precious right" of communication with his fellow men. The claim of freedom was thus presented on the basis of a norm of personal right, without regard to social utility. And by giving standing to the Literary Society in the case, the Council of State implicitly accepted the idea of such a norm. By this reasoning, limitations on free speech were represented as emanating and evolving from considerations of immediate public interest rather than from considerations of essential democratic rights. Such rights the Council of State had to mention, of course. But the implication of the decision is that these rights were in no way to be considered the creatures of the courts themselves.[12]

To put this principle in other terms, we may say that Council of State limited the public's interest to its immediate material order. Benjamin's right to speak in Nevers was upheld independently of his own obviously political intentions or Nevers' understanding of those intentions. Police powers were defined in terms of the mayor's duty, circumstances permitting, of giving every man his personal freedom, not his rights of citizenship.

But if this was so, how may claims of utility ever be weighed in the judicial balance? To a French public official reading the Council of State's decision in Benjamin's case, the answer would have appeared in the following phrase: "The possibility (*éventualité*) of disorder, as asserted by the Mayor" did not present "such a degree of gravity (*un tel degré de gravité*) as to render impossible the maintenance of order by other police measures. . . ." And lest public officials did not grasp the precise implication of this statement, the *commissaire du gouvernement* spelled out the details in his *conclusions* by showing that Mayor Herriot had once been quite successful in containing public disorder in Lyons where Benjamin had earlier spoken by the simple expedient of assigning more police to the area where his talk had taken place.

What else was the Council of State doing, in effect, than to follow a principle Justice Holmes had once proposed in the United States Supreme Court, that the test to be applied in

33

deciding whether a restriction on free speech was constitutional should be one of a "clear and present danger" of evils any legitimately constituted government is responsible for preventing?[13] Was not the Council simply saying that the Mayor of Nevers had not proved his plea that Benjamin's speech would have constituted a "clear and present danger" to Nevers' public order?

The apparent similarity of content masks the essential difference of form. For the very notions of immediate time and place so central to the application of a clear and present danger approach are in the French legal system formally criteria of *administrative* actions—of the use of police powers—alone. The idea that the same approach could be used to determine the criminal or civil liability of a private person who failed to censor his own remarks in the face of a clear and present danger not wholly of his own making has in fact no counterpart in French law.

In the logic of that law, such usage would be like holding a man guilty of spreading cholera, and would mean no more protection to the public, any more than the exercise of police powers has to do with the guilt or innocence of private persons. Their sole function in law is to maintain the physical appearance of public order. And their sole means of action is to prevent or ward off danger before harm occurs.[14] In administrative law, prior restraint of a speaker or writer therefore no more implies a moral judgment on the speaker than would a public quarantine aimed at preventing the spread of an epidemic. And if any particular act of prior restraint is challenged, it will have to be justified before the administrative courts in terms of the possible physical danger generated by the specifics of an interaction between speaker and audience rather than by reference to the speaker's intent.

Let me illustrate this peculiarity of French administrative law with two more recent court cases. Take first the *conclusions* of *Commissaire* Letourneur in a 1951 case before the Council of State that involved an order of the Prefect of the Vendée banning all public display of the journal, *Aspects de la France*, edited by remnants of Maurras' *Action française*. In pleading against the legality of this particular exercise of the police powers, Letourneur argued:

> All solutions of a general nature must be avoided; it is a question of measure, of understanding the circumstances of time and place. In any case, the idea of public order is uncertain; in fact it covers several notions: public movement, public calm, public safety. These notions correspond to the more or less imperative necessities of life in society; the requirement of maintaining order in the street is more essential, for example, than that of assuring quiet, and may therefore legitimately authorize more important restrictions [on civil liberties].
>
> In sum, Gentlemen [of the Court], in order to bring about the reconciliation between respect for public liberties and the duty of maintaining public order that is required of you, you are led, on the one hand, to adopt fine distinctions, susceptible of variation in relation to the liberty in question, the nature of the public interest to be safeguarded, and the necessities of time and place. Conversely, you are led to condemn all general and permanent [police] regulations, because [they] would fly in the face of the principle . . . according to which liberty is the rule and restriction the exception, and would therefore exceed the limits of legitimate police authority, limits which are determined by the necessity of maintaining order in a given place at a given time.[15]

Further evidence of the administrative law approach taken by the Council of State to problems of the relations between morals and the public order can be found in the *Société Franco-London* . . . case, decided on appeal by the Council in 1966.[16] The controversy arose when the Mayor of Nice banned throughout the commune the showing of a recent film. Distributors of the film immediately brought suit before the *tribunal administratif* of Nice to have the ban lifted. But the Mayor won his case in the lower court, on the argument that projection of the film in Nice "would be likely, by reason of the film's immoral character and local conditions, to lead to serious troubles and to be prejudicial to the public order." The distributors then appealed to the Council of State for relief, setting forth their own view of the correct relationship of morals to public order. It is critical to my thesis here to see how the *commissaire du gouvernement* urged the Council of State to decide the issue:

> Appellants argue that prohibition of a film can be justified only where there exists the possibility of a material and public disorder of such gravity that the mayor cannot insure maintenance of the peace by the ordinary means at his disposal. It is also claimed that where the only harm derived from showing the film might be to the moral order, such a threat cannot justify prohibition. . . .

> In this respect, appellants rework for their own use the very serious objections in law and in fact to the very idea of a public moral order, taken by my eminent predecessor, M. Mayras, an idea so difficult to grasp, so dangerous to invoke, and so delicate to apply. . . .

> In asking that the power of mayors to prohibit be limited only to those cases where serious material disorders for the control of which the police may not be adequate, appellants are really proposing—and they do not deny it— that you apply the rule of your decision in the *Benjamin* case concerning freedom of public meetings. Now, Gentlemen, as has often been pointed out, it cannot be said that the showing of movies, which is subject to ministerial authorization, has the character of a public liberty similar to that of freedom of meeting, or deserves the same protection.

> We attach too much importance to the juridical body of public freedoms and to the totality of their legal and jurisprudential guarantees to extend their benefit lightly or without serious consideration to other activities which the legislator himself has not consecrated.

> To raise public spectacles, and notably movies, to the level of public meetings, [when the latter] constitute an

essential element of democracy, would in fact be to lower the [status of public liberties].

In the second place, the alleged standardization of mores for which television may be responsible does not appear to us to be sufficient, in and of itself, to throw doubt on the basic principles of your previous ruling.[17]

In this respect, appellants' brief quits the ground of the material order and consents to become engaged on the difficult field of public morality. It hopes to convince you that this public morality is henceforward a national, uniform thing, and that the ministerial control commission which is responsible for delivering the *visa d'exploitation* for a film is alone capable of grasping it. From this it would follow that there is no place for judgment on the part of any mayor.

In express terms, the appeal invites us to have the law bow before the sociological fact of the standardization of mores under the influence of television, leaving us individually to deplore this development or not as we choose. How old a problem, indeed! And who is more familiar with it than judges like yourselves, and who have more often been able to resolve it, or more wisely?

The law will bow only before evidence of a new fact which throws doubt on some basic principle. Television probably does tend to standardize mores. But we doubt whether this phenomenon can be easily measured, or that it is simply proportional to the sale of television sets. In other times the same consequences must have been attributed to printing, the railroad, the automobile; and this may help us to realize how imprudent it is to speculate about effects of a given means or technique of expression on people's minds.

For a long time yet, we believe, cultural and moral diversities will continue to subsist within the confines of even one national community, and even of its regions, especially now that economic and cultural progress, and even administrative evolution, is tending toward the revitalization of the various regions in order that a true decentralization may be realized. All this means that it is not only desirable but probable that Lille and Perpignan, Strasbourg and Brest, will never receive this or that movie, or any other fruit of the human mind and spirit, in the same manner.

As to the fact that television presents films whose prohibition in this or that place you have authorized, it is without bearing on the body of your judgments. The use of television is a family matter. We personally think it does its harm less by its portrayal of eroticism than by its portrayal of violence. But in any case it is within the intimacy of the home and by the authority of the family that its influence is, or at least ought to be, felt. And those organizations that are especially zealous in defense of modesty have every encouragement to exercise their influence on those who are in charge of television. But this aspect of the problem lies wholly outside the matter of municipal administration which concerns us here.

Between a solution which would give mayors discretionary powers of judgment in these matters, and another that would provide film producers complete impunity, you have preferred an intermediary position which, though satisfying neither the one nor the other, accords with the general interest.

This formula appears to us sufficiently flexible and strong to serve as a framework which will allow for the future evolution of mores without opening the way to complete license.

Without putting the principles of your previous ruling in question, you can thereby refine your review. The present case furnishes the occasion. This is a supplementary reason for refusing to make the reversal you are being invited to make. We shall follow the appeal now on its subsidiary ground.

A preliminary matter can be disposed of immediately: that part of the Mayor's decree which invoked the risk of serious disorder. The *tribunal administratif* of Nice accepted this allegation, but it is supported in no other way. The municipality brings it up again before this Court, but somewhat timidly, by reference to the two letters which the Mayor received from the family organizations a short time before he imposed the prohibition. These letters express an intention on the part of the two groups to display their indignation concretely by sabotaging projection of the film. Gentlemen, these conventional threats, contrasting so markedly with the peaceful dispositions of most fathers, whether taken individually or in association, give a wretched idea of the manner in which the two organizations conceive of their influence and the appropriate means of exercising it. They seem to think that in order to demonstrate their opposition to the film they may use the very same violence which they are so quick to accuse in the young.

None of this is serious. The City of Nice provides no evidence whatsoever that could allow us to view these protests as anything other than a banal manifestation of a narrow and panicky corporatism.

It remains to deal with the danger of a direct threat to the public order considered from the moral point of view. Here we know that your rulings require the conjuction of two conditions: The threat must result both from the immoral character of said film and from local conditions. In this respect, the Mayor and the *tribunal administratif* have raised two questions whose materiality we must now treat. The materiality of these questions is contested at every point by plaintiffs.

Let us talk first, Gentlemen, of the immorality of the film. Your decisions have recognized the legitimacy, under condition of your review, of a mayor's judgment on this subject. We believe your rulings can be rendered more precise on this matter by stating that the review is in fact of a dual kind:

—you may judge of the circumstances in which the mayor has exercised his judgment and the evidence on which it is based;

—you may, furthermore, - and this is not the least delicate part of your role - confront his judgment with that which you yourselves have made on the basis of the evidence presented.

39

Now, whether on first instance or on appeal, the Mayor of Nice has been extremely discreet concerning both proof of the film's immorality and the evidence which he took as making it so.

It is agreed that on the date he took the decision to prohibit the showing of the film, the Mayor based his decision exclusively:

—on the movie's newspaper advertising, which can certainly be characterized as titillating;

—on the sentiments put forth by the two organizations representing [the interests of] family life.

Only a year later did the Mayor go to the trouble of organizing a private showing of the movie, and then only under the pressure of having to present his case before the *tribunal administratif* at Nice.

And as for getting the Mayor's view of the film's moral attributes,—a view that turns out to be rather elliptical, by the way—we have had to wait until the cause came before this Court.

In these circumstances it looks to us as though the Mayor's judgment on the question of the movie's morality was, at the time when the litigation began, based on insufficient familiarity with the facts of the matter. We could almost stop right here, then, and decide simply on the ground that his decision fails on its merits.

But you have seen the film yourselves, Gentlemen, and can therefore verify whether the Mayor's view is justified.

We are offered the spectacle of a certain number of beings of diverse age and both sexes who are, with one exception, engaged in the comedy of love and in endlessly taking advantage of one another about their respective feelings and intentions. The prize in this ballet turns out to be a sum of money which is passed from hand to hand. Blackmail, suicide, abortion, and the elementary techniques of conning take the place of what in earlier times constituted the often diabolical grace of *marivaudage*. Virtue here appears as but a by-product of naivete or cynicism. Childhood itself is presented as characterized by trickery and vulgarity, and this is not the least painful aspect of the matter. The only visible moral of the story is that animals are more dependable in their behavior than human beings. As for the rest, "he is the greater sucker who believes himself the cleverer (*tel est pris qui croyait prendre*)."

Taine once commented on *Cosi fan tutte* by noting that although everyone on stage lies, the music never does. In the case of this film, however, the art composing its comedy is, to our eyes, so gross and vulgar that it enjoins above all an irresistible reaction of mediocrity and staleness. There is no Mozart or Da Ponte here to save the production or to rejoice the viewer's spirit.

If after some cataclysm this work were to be the only remaining witness of our age, Gentlemen, we should have no occasion to be proud.

But as to the immorality of the movie—which our own personal opinion asserts without our even bothering to seek balance—is it really of the same nature that led you to apply the ruling of the *Films Lutêtia* case?

We think not. We don't see what harm this film can do by itself. To the perverse it can teach nothing; they will only laugh at its naive vulgarity. Among the virtuous it will only cause disgust. And as to the indifferent, they will likely suffer, at worst, profound boredom.

In any case, the story has an indirect moral: ultimately it is edifying about this age in which although we are allegedly all suckers it is still impossible to fool everyone all the time, as Abraham Lincoln remarked, and it is equally so about the moral disarray of youth without a cause.

Let me add that the film has no openly shocking or provocative scenes so far as public morality is concerned. Above all, it has no pictures of violence. At most a vague shadow of furtive eroticism, hardly worth mentioning, hangs over everything, everyone.

Under these circumstances the immorality of the film in the legal sense of the term does not appear to have been established.

As to local conditions, the record is highly instructive here as well.

When you introduced this idea in [your] decision of

December 18, 1959, most legal commentary regarded it as hardly more than a clause of style, leaving virtually nothing to get hold of . . . Your subsequent decisions have proved the contrary, for they have shown the precise sense of the term: [only proof of] protests emanating from very different social milieux, or some special composition of the given town's inhabitants, can justify the banning. The absence of such elements therefore deprives an interdiction of all legal foundation, even though it may bear on a film whose immoral character you are willing to grant.

If it is understandable why the City of Nice took little trouble in the first case (*Films Lutétia*) to be precise about the nature of the local conditions at a time when you were less exigent, we must note that in the instant case it is hardly more explicit than it was then.

The protests prior to the banning do not emanate from the "most diverse milieux," to use your terminology, but only the *Union départementale des Associations familiales* and an affiliate group, *La Ligue des Familles nombreuses*. They represent, Gentlemen, but a piece of public opinion.

As for the Prefect, whose comments have been approved and transmitted to you by the Minister of the Interior, he supposes that reference to a recrudescence of juvenile delinquency in the *Alpes-Maritimes* (the *département* of which Nice is the largest city) is enough. But since there is nothing explicit about this assertion, you can only put it aside.

Neither in the record nor elsewhere do we find any evidence which could lead us to think that the inhabitants of Nice displayed, as of 1960, any characteristics suggesting that they had to be specially protected from this film.

Local conditions were therefore not of the kind which could furnish legal foundation for the prohibitory measure.

Let us note finally that at no time did the City of Nice respond to the very subsidiary argument of appellants, to the effect that the Mayor at most might properly have forbidden to minors of 18 years or less.

Thus, Gentlemen, none of the conditions which might have justified an interdiction of the film's showing has been met here. The danger of material disorder must be forthwith discarded. As to an indirect attack on the public order, we do not find in this cause, either in the film's immorality or in local conditions, the requisite conjunction. It is sufficient, indeed, to find the absence of but one of these elements. We therefore propose that you base your decision exclusively on the absence of the necessary local conditions, leaving aside thereby the question of the film's immorality, and this for two reasons:

—On the one hand, the record is particularly light on this matter of local conditions, and we believe it would be useful to underline the duty of municipal authorities' being prepared to explain themselves fully on this point when they come to court.

—On the other hand, we think it desirable whenever possible that you avoid pronouncing yourselves explicitly as to the moral qualities of a particular film. You know, of course, how much of the subjective must enter into any such judgment. In addition, however, we think you have no duty to furnish film producers any patents, whether of morality or immorality, from which they could draw commercial advantages.

For these reasons, we conclude in favor of annulling the judgment under appeal and the decision of the Mayor of Nice, dated March 2, 1960, with expenses for the first instances and the appeal alike being placed at the charge of the City of Nice.

So in spite of his argument that films are not entitled to the same legal forms of protection as freedom of press and association, and his maintaining a right of moral censorship on the part of the Council of State, the *commissaire du gouvernement* nevertheless urged that decision in the instant case be made on the same basis as that of the Benjamin case. He was asserting, in brief, that the administrative law perspective on public order must include but a vanishingly small moral component.

We are thus now brought to the following question: if French legal practice treats clear and present dangers as criteria for judgment in administrative courts on the use of police powers for maintenance of the material order alone, what approach will the ordinary courts take in determining civil or criminal liability where the legal question must be the guilt or negligence of the private speaker or writer? For the formal distinction between prior censorship by public officials and deterring expressions of harmful views by private persons by means of the threat of criminal sanctions implies the elaboration and the maintenance of two different sets of jurisprudential principles, appropriate respectively to public policing on the one hand, and private, "self-policing" on the other.

Now to be held criminally or civilly liable for breaking one of the various laws regarding free speech means that you have deliberately or negligently used words to cause injury. There are therefore two broad conditions which have to be met before civil or criminal liability may be imposed upon a speaker or writer. There must be some specific harm done (or the expression must coincide with a predetermined list of opinions whose expression is considered harmful in and of itself). And the court must discover in the words used either a conscious purpose on the part of the author to do the certain harm, or a sufficient negligence on his part to justify his civil liability. This is to say that an author can be found responsible in theory only when his malice, bad will, or guilty intent—or in civil cases, his negligence—has been determined by the court independently of its determination of the harm caused, while the actual harm must be found to have been caused without reference to his bad will. In this way, the determination whether sanctions are to be applied in free speech cases corresponds formally to the means employed in any other type of civil or criminal case.

But this formal similarity masks a profound difference between free speech acts and other kinds, resulting from the difficulty of determining the real harm caused by words independently of the motive attributed to him who uses them. Certainly we should not wish to punish a man for his bad will alone so long as that bad will found no apparent and outward expression. On the other hand, we should not want to punish a man for some actual harm caused by his words if we knew that he had spoken them with all the good will in the world. But if the alleged *corpus delicti* is an idea or opinion, can we really distinguish between the putative harm its public expression does and the putative intent of its author? Hence wherever in French law a person is expected to police his own remarks under the threat of legal sanctions, the judges of the ordinary courts are brought face to face with the relationships between intent and circumstances.

If such relationships were simply objective, as many libertarians would certainly like them to be, judges would have little need for "subtle intuitions." No constitutional order would be made up of anything more than the formal statements defining it, and all possible meanings would lie on the surface of statutory language itself. But no simply logical description of social practices can bear every meaning felt by those who experience them. So in free speech cases attributions of intent reflect the character given by courts and judges to the community itself, and the rituals of the courts frame dramas whose actors often mirror a people's deepest feelings about the nature of their society.

In the absence of a clear list of *délits d'opinion*, of ideas, that is, whose public expression, without regard to circumstances, is always considered harmful taken as prima facie evidence of guilty intent, statutory rules by themselves provide only the sketchiest of guides to the practical work of the regularly courts. Their discovery of intent (*scienter*) involves far more subtle processes than laying statutory language and the words under indictment on the table together to see if there is an overlap. For although one may perhaps speak in the abstract of a minimum content of moral law necessary and sufficient to a community,[18] in any real social context this minimum potentially interpenetrates many other and subtler rules of thought and conduct. The relationship of the words to the circumstances in which they were spoken is therefore, just as Holmes said, central to an appreciation of the ideas they express.

It is at this point that the formally antirevolutionary impulse of the French legal system and the principles of 1789 confront each other. A kind of modus vivendi has been struck between the abstract universal principles of the Revolution and the immemorial practices and traditions of the courts, in which the former take on practical effect only insofar as they are mediated through the latter in actual litigation. This is not merely to observe cynically that in practice judges give more weight to existing social forces than to justice. It is, rather, to say that if the courts did not have formal ways of recognizing the demands made by these forces, principles would have no content in practice.

The "circumstances" to which the ordinary courts in France give due are therefore of a different order, as we shall see, than those taken into account by the administrative courts. They are derived in effect from a sense of moral conventions, framed by universal rules, like the Declaration of Rights, but fleshed out by the ethical conceptions of a wide variety of particular communities—geographical, professional, and work. Thus, though the nominal frame of reference of the ordinary courts in France is "positive" in a verbal sense, because it is constituted of written rules, the laws' application depends essentially on the meaning of facts identified as such by community mores.[19]

As a consequence, the legal history of the twentieth century Republics in the realm of free speech has been characterized by an implicit claim of the ordinary courts to provide ultimate definitions of the difference between a lawful and unlawful consciousness. I do not mean to say that the ordinary courts have seen it as their job to create law itself. They have attempted, rather, to define boundaries between legitimate and illegitimate states of mind. They have taken materials offered them by the community outside the courtroom and filtered these through their own processes to arrive at statements of the differences between the guilty and innocent will. But the processes by which they have arrived at these statements have an irreducible institutional element in them; for no more in French courts than in others are such processes neutral. The well-nigh universal interest in how courts work stems precisely from the ways in which they recognize, or refuse to recognize, the world outside the courtroom, and the ways in which they weigh the elements they do recognize.

This study will show in particular that the French civil and criminal courts are not simply tolerant. Unlike those of the Council of State, their judges will be found committed to viewpoints beyond those involved in defense of an immediate order. It is when we see their decisions as statements of moral perspective, sanctioning principles they believe antithetical to the meaning of justice, that we can appreciate their interest as commentaries on the nature of the social order in its moral aspects.

The French legal system taken in its dual character thus operates institutionally under the stress of thinking in free speech cases that is at once liberal and democratic—liberal because it regards the function of law as maintaining those fences which allow each man to enjoy his rights without infringing on the equal rights of his fellows, and democratic because it regards the law as the ultimate expression of the community's life and meaning. If the individual's right to speak and his righteousness in speaking can thereby be distinguished, they cannot be altogether separated. As soon as we feel that no man can be wholly justified simply by outward adherence to the institutions, customs, works, and logic of his particular time and place, we open the possibility of his making claims against the group and the group's making claims against him. Prosecutions undertaken in the name the Republic since 1881 have had, in other words, to try to take the moral measure of citizenship, while the administrative courts, with a fine indifference to ideas, have merely tried to protect outward order on the other.

I conclude, then, pointing to the differences between the administrative and ordinary courts—their respective personnel, modes of reasoning procedures, and objects of decision—in terms of a fundamental duality of the French legal system's understanding of distinctions between law and order. Order is constituted of certain immediately utilitarian or expediential considerations that can be threatened by observable "clear and present dangers" of a contingent or accidental kind. Order is thus in the French view properly protected by police action, whose appropriate mode is preventive and therefore, in the realm of speech, necessarily a matter of prior restraint. It is up to the State as administrative apparatus to keep the fences up.

And so appeals from the practical actions of police officials can be taken only after the fact to the administrative courts, whose judgments are aimed at creating among public officials a sense of responsibility appropriate to this kind of peace keeping. In this respect, we can now see the Benjamin case as more than a leading one in administrative law. It is nothing less than a symbol of one aspect of an archetype of French society.

The other side of this archetype is symbolized by the work of the regular criminal and civil courts, whose function in matters of free speech is to define the positive moral content of law. Though judgments of the regular courts sometimes do reflect a particular Government's policies, and prosecutions often seem politically motivated in this narrow sense, they also more broadly serve to identify a regime as an historical phenomenon which all are agreed needs legitimation in the realm of principle as well as in that of goods and services. By undertaking prosecutions against speech acts, many of which in themselves hardly constitute a threat to the Republic or its institutions, the State shows that it means to take its own supposed principles seriously. In so doing, it of course does more: it gives dignity to the voices of critics, a dignity derived from a ritual combat of which the courts serve as one of the cockpits. And it is this combat itself which expresses a deeper truth than can be captured by any positive institution by itself.

Later on in the study I shall present some examples and an analysis of this ritual. For the moment, it is important to point out that the differences between forms of action and modes of reasoning incorporated by the dual court system, with their different ways of attributing responsibility for the maintenance of order and law respectively, came into existence without reference to any formal constitution so far as free speech is concerned. The fact that contemporary analysis has formally distinguished between the two components of the legal system by assigning them the names of *régime préventif* and *régime répressif* need not mislead us here. It is true that the antecedents of the administrative law system can be traced back to the first Napoleonic period, to the *conseils du roi* of the *ancien régime*, and from thence to features of administration dating back at least as far as the sixteenth century.[20] But even today no written constitution of France has ever dealt explicitly with the system of dual jurisdictions, which has simply evolved, though not without some opposition, of its own accord. It would therefore appear that the problem of maintaining "a constant connection between what right permits and interest demands," as Rousseau phrased it, has been the very problem governing fundamental perceptions of the French political and legal classes over the past three of four centuries. What is then remarkable about French legal processes in the realm of free speech today is not merely that the intentions of the authors of the Press Law of 1881 should have become overlain with usages which they meant to reject, but that these usages should so strongly reflect an historical pattern in which relations between the two aspects of the maintenance of order, preventive and repressive, while always marked by attempts at their formal reconciliation, should at the same time reflect their inherent and perpetual conflict.

Appreciation of the forces tending toward maintenance of this conflict requires, however, some review of the work of 1881, of the ideas motivating the authors of the Press Law, and of the push of events since that time. We will then better understand why the writing of a formal charter of freedom of speech and press in 1881, which at first seemed a dramatic turning of the page in the story of French constitutionalism, has turned out to have far more ambivalent consequences than its authors intended.

CHAPTER TWO

Genesis and Evolution
of the Press Law

The free communication of thoughts and opinions is one of
the most precious rights of man. Every citizen may henceforward speak, write, and publish freely, except to answer
for the abuse of this liberty in those cases determined by the
law.

Article II, *The Declaration of the Rights of Man*, 1789

Those who drafted the Declaration's article on free speech
evidently shared Blackstone's view of the matter: a man must
censor himself under some conditions to avoid criminal or
civil sanctions. This view was taken to be the basic principle
of liberty in 1789, and was clearly reflected in the parliamentary
debates leading up to passage of France's contemporary charter
of free speech, the Press Law of July 29, 1881. And since this
view seems to preclude official prior restraint on speech, we may
suppose that the legislators of 1881 generally repudiated it too
—especially with memories of the Second Empire still fresh in
their minds. And yet when the Benjamin case was decided in
1933, administrative law clearly admitted the principle of prior
restraint by public officials, reserving for the administrative
courts only the question whether this or that act of censorship
had been legitimately engaged in under the immediate circumstances. How did such a development come about?

Historically speaking, it is a development related to the division between private and public law that goes back into the
legal and political institutions of the Old Regime. But it is not

the history of the matter at this point which concerns us now. It is rather the logic of it. And to get at this logic nothing will serve better than to review the 1881 debates themselves. For in these debates we shall see a fundamental conflict—felt but not wholly worked out—between the idea of personal liability as the basic instrument of public order, and that of police action. To study these debates now is to understand how the legislators of 1881 neither grasped the momentum of the past nor guessed the potential of their own ambivalence. Like many another cornerstone, in short, the Press Law of 1881 did not determine the appearance of the building.

This was probably inevitable. All assertions, declarations, and statements aiming at human liberty have something vain about them, a vanity sooner or later revealed by events. And as the authors of the Press Law were aiming at a general liberty we should sooner pity than mock their efforts. Yet the Press Law of 1881 hardly represented the first effort in French history to establish a statutory regime of free speech: 1789, 1814, and 1848 could make certain claims too. And in the face of the withering of these earlier efforts we may wonder that the legislators of 1881 could suppose the effective establishment of free speech was to be undertaken primarily by the abrogation of most of the repressive legislation from the past.[1] Revolutionary habits of thinking seem to have obscured the real difficulties of their task.

That the age was beset with revolutionary problems the uprising of the Paris Commune had shown. But the legislators of 1881 seem in many respects to have fought the causes of 1789 again, perhaps even more than those of 1848, rather than the new ones of their own age. So though the Press Law of 1881, and some of the *fin de siècle* liberal legislation of which it is one of the key pieces, may be said to be formally on the side of such principles of 1789 as liberty and equality, we must nevertheless recognize that these principles were seen from the perspective of a social order in which the legal protection of acquired property rights came first.[2] The functional order which even the most radical legislators were prepared to envisage in 1881 consisted essentially of small proprietors, whose individual rights were based on or an extension of their independent holdings, and where even the idea of laisser faire was seriously limited by an underlying demand for protectionism. Belief in the abstract merits of *liberté, egalité, fraternité* was tempered by the stoicism of the French middle-class spirit, thus characterized in a poet's lines:

> Avoir une maison commode, propre et belle,
> Un jardin tapissé d'espaliers odorants,
> Des fruits, d'excellent vin, peu de train, peu d'enfants;
> Régler tous ses desseins sur un juste modèle,
> Dire son chapelet en cultivant ses entes. . . .
> Et attendre chez soi bien doucement la mort.[3]

Perhaps as little as their descendants today was the Frenchman of the 1880s willing to believe that the future, left to itself, would "naturally work out for the best."[4] Whether of Left or Right, whether Radicals, Liberals, Conservatives, to all intents and purposes they shared a common conviction that it was necessary, as Leon Gambetta said, to "apply positivism to the political order."[5] In effect, this meant that every individual should have a fence around himself and his property, a *situation acquise* in both the social and physical sense within which he was, as a passive subject, fully protected by the State from the possibility of aggression on the part of neighbors and fellow citizens.

The political and legal question was, how should the fences be defined and by whom should they be maintained? But this question turned out to involve a second and more paradoxical one especially critical for the constitutional implications of a press law: why should the laws of one age, or of one legislative session, have any more authority than those of succeeding ages, or sessions? The story of the Press Law in the twentieth century suggests in fact that every age and every legislature in France does have essentially constituent powers, derived both from the force of events and the "consent of the governed," and that in some ways these powers tend to mean in practice what the courts and judges have thought they meant, or what they think the felt necessities of the time seemed to require. The evolution of decisional law suggests the irony of the legal positivism of 1881 and, indeed, of the Revolution itself. For by its essentially deductive mode of political and legal thought, this positivism, which meant to change everything, succeeded instead in guaranteeing a particularly proprietary conservatism, whereby everything struggling to be born could only be seen as a threat to everything that already had legal existence.

Thus in retrospect it is easy to guess why the legislators of 1881 failed: for though all courts today take the Law of July 29, 1881 as point of departure in cases involving freedom of expression, it is equally true that they are part of a legal system built out of the past. Were a whole new class of lawyers to spring to life with every new statute, the manner of interpreting and applying the words and provisions of new statutes might then reflect the intentions of the legislature. But lawyers came into this world before legislators, and their ways with words are older. How noble, and how naive, then, was the intent of Article 68 of the Press Law:

> Are abrogated all edicts, laws, decrees, ordinances, decisions, rules and whatever declarations generally that concern printing, bookselling, the periodical and non-periodical press, hawking, posting, selling on the public thoroughfare, and that concern the crimes and delicts provided for by the laws on the press and other means of publication, without, however, bringing back into force any provisions that have been abrogated by previous laws.[6]

Today, one can only say that the inclusion of this article under the heading "*Dispositions Transitoires*" was appropriate in a way which the legislators of 1881 could hardly have appreciated.

The regulation of freedom of expression since 1881 must indeed be traced in three different kinds of developments. First, there has been the development of administrative law and its relationship to statutory controls, which will be touched on again in the next chapter. Second, there have been statutory additions and modifications of the Press Law itself; these are outlined in the latter part of this chapter. And finally, there have been the judicial interpretations of key phrases in the Press and related laws; and as for this element, we must say that the period since 1881 has not so much brought about an evolution in law as it has displayed certain tendencies of interpretation. These tendencies are illustrated in Chapter IV.

If one may say of the Press Law that it was perhaps the greatest of the grand series of statutory acts giving legal definition to the Third Republic, he would nevertheless have to add in the next breath that this particular attempt at definition was notable chiefly for its breadth. The parliamentary regime which produced it—the one destined to last longer than all the other regimes of France's post-Revolutionary history to date—was born and nourished on paradoxes, the most fundamental of which were to find implicit expression in the Press Law itself. To put the constitutional situation briefly, seldom in history can such strong sentiment in favor of a positive state among so many classes have thrown up in practice a more self-effacing system of government.

This paradox is easily explained: agreement on positive forms in theory meant strong disagreement on content in practice. The Third Republic was allowed to exist because, as its principal founder, Adolphe Thiers, once noted, it divided Frenchmen the least. Its three so-called Constitutional Laws of 1875 were finally voted only under pressure of fear of new disorders comparable to those that had occurred four years previously in the Paris Commune. And the major characteristic of these laws was that they could have been adapted to almost any kind of regime —parliamentary, presidential, monarchical. It is not that their authors inadvertently failed to deal with most of the fundamental questions about the general order that constitutions must either provide for or assume to be already answered. They did their best, rather, to avoid deciding them. The Third Republic thus started life with little of the moral or intellectual authority appropriate to the governance of a people whose professed national aspirations were revolutionary but whose real demands were for order. Though the "provisional rules of morality" reflected in the civil and commercial codes had the support of substantial proportions of nearly all classes, the Constitutional

Laws left almost blank the vision of France which was to guide the reconstruction of political life from the bits and pieces inherited from her earlier political history. In the 1870s there were very few reasons to suppose that the Third Republic would long survive infancy.

As a product of that infancy, the Press Law itself was also inevitably compromised. Had the dominant forces in the Assembly at the time been monarchists it is doubtful there would have been any new law at all. But the legislative elections of 1876 had produced at least a negative majority in the legislature. When first elected, this majority was dedicated to one proposition: that the office of the Presidency, then occupied by General Macmahon, should not be allowed to develop its monarchic, or, as we should probably say today, its presidential potential. The formal turning point came in the crisis of May 16, 1877, when MacMahon called for the resignation of Prime Minister Simon and, following a dispute with the Chamber of Deputies about the naming of Simon's successor, dissolved the Chamber to call for new elections. The republicans won a clear victory in those elections, and this victory was in a measure repeated two years later in elections to the Senate. The stage was thus set for an attempt to give the Third Republic a more republican constitutional structure than had theretofore been possible.

This scene did not last long. It was largely changed with the death of its principal actor, Gambetta, in 1882. From then on it became a matter of the Republic's attaining what characteristics it was to show through the force of passing events, notably the Dreyfus Affair and the First World War. Its constitution could be said to be evolving even on the Republic's deathbed in 1940. But 1881 was nevertheless to leave its mark when, under the leadership of Gambetta, a majority hammered out in the first half of that year the Press Law.

Gambetta's parliamentary followers were largely made up in this instance of a group which history has come to call the Opportunists. The smaller part were so-called Radicals. The Opportunists were generally what one would expect of nineteenth-century liberals. They believed in a strong state where repression of crime and protection of property were concerned, but they repudiated any idea of public social welfare. Their support of freedom of speech reflected mostly sentiments of a kind of progressive utilitarianism at the core of which lay an idea of salvation by positive science. The Radicals, on the other hand, reflected Jacobin views of 1789 more strongly, which is to say that their petit bourgeois interests were overlain with populist sentiments. They believed in the inseparability of the idea of France as a nation and that of human rights.

The conflict of Opportunists and Radicals largely dominated the legislative debates on the Press bill. The theme of the Opportunist, or Liberal, position lay in what the *rapporteur* of the special house committee appointed to draft the measure called the "reconciliation" of two general principles—"liberty, principle of natural right; responsibility, principle of social order."[7] The emphasis on "responsibility" is what distinguished the Liberal position most clearly from that of the Radicals. What the former meant, of course, was criminal liability; the Liberal approach to the subject was dictated by the assumption that any reasonable man who knew he could be held criminally liable for his words would think carefully before he spoke dangerous thoughts. The connection between "responsibility" and "social order" was to be made by the utilitarian one of graduated pains and pleasures— legal pains and social rewards.

Of the arsenal of weapons upon which the public authorities of France had historically drawn to suppress freedom of speech —registration of publishers, printers, booksellers, prior censorship, deposits of caution money, and criminal liability—it was therefore really only the last which the Liberals wanted to retain. Their own recent experience had taught them as much. From the earlier history of the Second Empire, they remembered well enough the suppression of their own press when Napoleon III had wanted to demonstrate his populist sympathies. But when he had decided to "constitutionalize" his regime under Liberal pressure in 1868-69, he did so by allowing criminal prosecutions against outspoken detractors of his policies and regime to be substituted for censorship and caution money. This change proved to be especially favorable to Liberal interests and political ambitions. The often spectacular press trials it engendered offered both Liberals and some of the more extreme opposition groups a means of propaganda they were often able to turn to political advantage.[8] Failing to draw any new lesson from the downfall of MacMahon, the Liberals wanted essentially the continuation of the regime under which they had prospered politically twelve years earlier.

Yet as the Liberals looked to history in drafting the Press Law bill, so also did the Radicals. Their view of it was, of course, rather different. As opposed as the Opportunists to censorship and caution money, they wanted to reject even special criminal liability for press offenses. Their basic argument was a populist one; only the People [they insisted] were able to maintain public order, as this passage from a parliamentary speech by one of their spokesmen suggests:

> It's a good thing that public opinion has taken on the burden of protecting the general interests of the State, the reputations of private citizens and political figures alike . . . [and] the common patrimony of our political parties. It's a good thing public opinion is taking care of these things because judicial repression must inevitably fail at them. . . . To those publishers who deserve authority and confidence, the public gives authority and confidence. Democracy accepts them, listens to them, and takes their views into account. As for those who deserve less confidence, whether the People reads them or not, it has no faith in them, and does not accept their point of view. . . . This is the truth! This is how our morals have been transformed, this is how public order is truly guaranteed! For Heaven's sake, gentlemen (smiles on the Right), don't wreck this fine thing. Don't go and make a repressive law.[9]

On more nearly jurisprudential grounds, the Radical argument insisted that to make criminal offenses of certain kinds of speech would controvert the accepted legal definition of a crime. This definition consisted of three criteria: malicious intent, explicit damage to society, and the existence of incriminating facts. A Radical spokesman found the first two criteria quite inapplicable to speech and writings:

There is a hopeless legal flimsiness in all prosecutions concerning the press, because one has to hunt around among all the possible courts and even dream up new ones in order to find judges whose minds are sufficiently supple to come to grips with human thought, and to uncover its real meaning beneath all the disguises it may wear. You must devise a court which exercises the true power of inquisition; . . . you have to go behind the thought itself in order to get at the motives on which its expression is based.[10]

In any event, the Radicals asked, could the threat of criminal punishment really serve to maintain order? Experience under the last years of the Second Empire suggested not. With the substitution of criminal prosecutions for censorship the virulence of the attacks on Napoleon III had in no way been moderated. On the contrary, the trials themselves had only given additional stimulus to social and political ferment.

In the light of this perspective the Radicals wanted the new Press Law to do only two things. The first and most important was to abrogate all previous laws, statutes, *ordonnances* and decrees on the subject. The second was to provide for the application of the so-called *droit commun*[11] to speech as to all other social relationships. By *droit commun*, they meant specifically two provisions, one from the criminal code and the other from the civil.[12] Article 60 of the criminal code defines material complicity, and Article 1382 of the civil code defines civil liability. Article 1382 reads:

Any act whatever by which one man causes an injury to another obliges him by whom the injury was caused to make reparation for it.

And Article 60 reads:

Will be punished as accomplices of an act defined as a crime or offense, whosoever, by gifts, promises, threats, abuse of authority or power, machinations or wrongful misrepresentations, provokes such an act or gives instructions to have it committed; Whosoever procures weapons, instruments, or any other means which serve the act, knowing that they serve the act; Whosoever consciously aids or abets the author or authors of the act, either in those matters which prepare or facilitate it, or in those which consummate it, without prejudice to the punishments specifically determined in this Code against the authors of plots or of provocations against the security of the State, even in those cases where the crime which it was the purpose of the conspirators or provacateurs to commit is not committed.

According to the Radicals, the virtue of Article 1382 of the Civil Code was that it took care of libel and slander, and thus the problem of actually identifying the occurrence of an injury. The virtue of Article 60 was that it wholly excluded the idea of moral complicity, and thus could never be used as a cover to reintroduce the detested *délits d'opinion* which had been the mark of earlier press law.[13] The Radicals thus proposed that the operative section of the Press Law, its Chapter Four, read simply as follows:

Article 1: There are no special offences of the press. Whosoever uses the press or any other means of publicizing his views is liable only according to the *droit commun.* . . .
Article 2: The display, sale, distribution, peddling, or advertising of any obscene object or publication will be punished by imprisonment. . . and fine.
Copies of such material put in public view, on sale, distributed or peddled will be seized and destroyed.

The Liberals' response to these arguments was broad, for their basic conviction was anti-populist. They did not believe any public to be capable of maintaining order on the basis of its own tastes and actions. As a consequence, they argued, the *droit commun* was inappropriate to control of the press. They believed its application must mean either an aggravation of punishments and restrictions, or none at all.[14] The codes had not been designed to deal with public communication and to try to make them serve such a purpose would be to enter upon an uncharted sea.[15] And were the Assembly to accept the Radical proposals, they argued, it would be abdicating its sovereign responsibilities to legislate. With nothing but the *droit commun* at hand, the courts would have to elaborate their own rules for the control of speech and press. The only possible result of such a state of affairs, said the Liberals, would be the recreation of the same state of affairs that had existed before 1870: a mass of regulations understood only by lawyers, and perhaps not even by them.[16] The Radical proposal would thus have created the illogical arrangement whereby all social relations except public communication were regulated by codes particular to the kind of relations in question. And this would mean, in turn, the probability of capricious prosecutions, inadequate to the long term maintenance of public order as well as unfair to speakers, authors, publishers, and editors.

In fact the Liberals thought the weakness of earlier legal controls was to be found not so much in their goals as in their confusions and complexities. These things worked not only against the innocent author or speaker by making him unsure of legal limits, but also against public order, because those with evil intentions could find ways and means of escaping through uncertain definitions of liability. As for the Radical argument that it was wrong to assimilate incitement to execution of a crime with the crime itself, the Liberals believed rather that such assimilation was crucial to any system of legally sanctioned responsibility. In their eyes, the problem was not to destroy the possibility of incrimination based on provocation. The problem was to define it with precision. In the words of a Liberal spokesman,

> Doesn't the Penal Code punish false news propagated with the purpose of upsetting confidence in public funds? Yet . . . especially in a country like ours, I do not believe that everything depends on the stability of money; . . . (It) has a considerable interest, of course, but the tranquility of the country, material interests aside, . . . depends

far more on certain broad moral matters of the highest importance, and it is certainly just as essential to protect these.

(As for the draft provisions concerning) "seditious cries": all we need do is to notice that the Penal Code punishes noises and disturbances of the peace at night. . . . Well, would you have the fellow who disturbs the sleep of a few citizens by singing an inoffensive song in the middle of the night exposed to prosecution . . . while the man who in the full light of day cries out a seditious phrase subverting, or perhaps capable of subverting, public safety, especially in the times we are now passing through, enjoys impunity? That would be inadmissible![17]. . . If one had to distinguish between the guilt of the agitator and the guilt of the agent, I would make it in favor of the agent. . . . A man who takes pen in hand or the platform at a public meeting may well abuse the powers of his talent . . . and push those of his readers or hearers who incline to credulity to commit an act whose criminal character is incontestable: Must we then hold responsible only those who would not have committed the crime but for the burning incitement poured upon them, while he who was the true author . . . is allowed to take refuge in a prudent abstention (from the deed itself), though perhaps present at the scene of the disaster and even at the scene of punishment of those whose only fault was to believe what they had been told or had read?

Does not ethics, does not reason, tell us to lay responsibility at least equally if not more at the door of him . . . who in the solitude of his room is able to reflect on the full meaning of his words and the consequences of his provocative exhortations and yet does not retreat from them in the face of the harm to society he is going to cause, nor in the face of the deplorable situation he is going to impose on those foolish enough to take his advice?[18]

To these moral arguments the Liberal Minister of Justice added the following political observations:

Here is a fact, a direct incitement: does it not show that its author had a malicious intent? Is not such an incitement intended to produce serious trouble in our society, to alarm social interests? Of course it is! If you leave incitement unpunished when its purpose is to bring about a crime defined by the *droit commun*, . . . then are you not allowing society to be profoundly harmed?

If the authorities of the law do not act, if the author of the incitement remains unpunished, won't the situation be continually aggravated by a probable increase of such activities? . . . What can the citizens do to protect themselves when they no longer feel the tutelary hand of society protecting them?[19]

For the Liberals, then, the proper solution to the problem of repressing incitement to criminal acts, without thereby limiting language of innocent intent, was to incorporate the idea of "direct" provocation in the Press Law. Only language which recommended a specific course of action in itself criminal would be punishable, and then only if the connection between the language and the criminal act it recommended was manifest. The relevant section of Chapter Four of the Press Law bill was thus to read:

Article 23: Will be punished as accomplice . . . whosoever, whether by speeches, cries, threats, . . . or writings or printed matter sold or distributed . . . in public places or meetings, or by notices of printed matter shown to public view, directly provokes the agent or agents to commit (a crime) if the provocation is followed by its effect. This provision shall also apply where the provocation is followed by an (unsuccessful) attempt, as provided for in Article 2 of Criminal Code.

Without faith in public opinion per se, however, the Liberals could not be satisfied by such a provision by itself. If public order were as much threatened by incitements as they seemed to believe, by far the greater effects of such provocation must be general and threatening to the moral atmosphere of society, rather than specific. They thus included in the next articles of Chapter Four two prohibitions that reflected in some measure the old *délits d'opinion*. But instead of making incitement to "disobedience of the laws" generally punishable, they drew up a definite list of felonies:

> Article 24: Whosoever, by any of the means enumerated in the preceding article, directly incites the felonies of murder, pillage, arson, or any of the felonies against the security of the State enumerated in Articles 75 through 101 of the Criminal Code, will be punished [even] in those cases where the incitement has not been followed by its effect. . . . Any seditious cry or song will [also] be punished. . . .

And in the same vain:

> Article 25: Any provocation by a means enumerated in Article 23, addressed to [members of the armed forces], for the purpose of dissuading them from the fulfillment of their military duties and the obedience they owe their commanders in all matters ordered for the execution of military laws and rules, will be punished. . . .

The rest of Chapter Four of the Press Law Bill dealt with special offenses. Article 26 punished (without defining) insult to the Chief of State, and Article 27 punished

> the publication, distribution or reproduction, by whatever means, of false news, forged documents, wrongly or mendaciously attributed to a third party, when, done in bad faith, it troubles public order, or is apt to trouble it. . . .

> The same acts will be punished [more heavily] when [they] are of a nature to impair discipline in the [armed forces] or hamper the war effort of the Nation.

And Article 28 revived another provision culled from earlier laws by providing that an

> Attack on good morals (*bonnes moeurs*) committed by one of the means enumerated in Articles 23 will be punished by imprisonment of from one month to two years and a fine of from ($3) to ($400).
>
> The same penalties will be imposed for offering in sale distributing, or displaying drawings, engravings, paintings, symbols or obscene statues. All examples of these . . . displayed in public, put on sale, hawked or distributed, will be seized.

When it came libel and slander (*délits contre les personnes*), the Liberals showed themselved to be no more of the Radicals' disposition than they had been in other matters. They adhered to the use of criminal rather than civil actions in defamation partly because, as *Rapporteur* Lisbonne argued, they believed authors likely to engage in defamatory language would seldom have enough money to satisfy civil damages.[21] But the more fundamental reason for the preference for public prosecution seems to have lain again in the Liberal feeling that public order depended wholly on a moral order whose conventions needed positive State protection. In keeping with this view they wished to prohibit the defense of the truth in defamation cases generally, on the ground that the purpose of criminal law in these matters must not be to reveal truth but to forestall public disturbances.

Throughout the debates on the Press Law the Liberals displayed, in short, a conception of French society in which the moral sentiments of the vast majority needed constant legal support by the "tutelary hand." All men needed to know just where they stood by statutory definition that good order in the broadest sense should prevail.

And yet implementation of this view has not been without irony, perhaps even to the point of strengthening sentiments of class conflict. For the harmonious society is evidently one in which litigiousness is reduced to a minimum. But the Liberal spirit involves constant prosecution for the sake of reassuring the majority of *bien-pensants* that their moral conventions are indeed being protected. At the same time, to make publishers liable before editors and authors, as the Press Law does, renders prosecutions against them risky on two counts. First, they are more likely to have adequate legal advice. And more fundamentally, such prosecutions only risk emphasizing that the conventions of society are touchy among the very classes of people who are supposed to be their most convinced defenders. The practical consequence has been that prosecutions inspired by the Liberal spirit have by and large fried only the smaller fish, and more often those on the Left, while at the same time generating a sense of hypocrisy in the system shared by virtually all classes alike.

The temptation to say contentious things was in any case stimulated by an original provision of the Press Law concerning jurisdictions and procedures. It is here that the new law made its greatest concessions to the Radical point of view. Before 1881, trials involving speech and press were generally heard before a panel of three judges sitting alone. From the state's point of view, these so-called *tribunaux correctionnels* had the great advantage of disposing of such cases rapidly and with a minimum of publicity. It was of course just this feature which the more ardent reformers of the previous system were most anxious to change. The 1881 Press Law therefore made provision for the general use of the *cours d'assises* instead of the *tribunaux correctionnels*, to insure defendants of a jury trial. The Radicals believed the jury trial to be absolutely indispensable to fairness in these matters because, they said, the value of an opinion necessarily varies with the times, and only a jury "drawn constantly from the People and returning to it" could provide a just estimate of the existence and degree of an offense created by words.[22] Given the greater complexity of procedures in the *cours d'assises*, these provisions of the law were at least favorable to the profession of barristers, if rather less so to that order of prudent citizens so dear to the hearts of the Opportunists.

The Press Law bill was ultimately passed on July 29, 1881,

in substantially the same form as that in which it had been drafted, with the Liberal point of view dominant. It opened the possibility of starting new journals, reviews, and periodicals to anyone who had the desire and the means to fulfill it, so long as he merely identified himself to the authorities. It not only did away with caution money and formal censorship, it looked as if it were going to do away with all the former complexities, obscurities, overlappings of statutes, jurisdictions, and procedures. The Press Law of 1881 might therefore be considered in the abstract, and was so considered at the time, as striking a blow for liberty and perhaps for order as well.[23]

Yet even in 1881 not everyone was happy with the new legislation. The most pessimistic of the liberatarians of the age prophesied that whatever the intention of the National Assembly had been, earlier law on the subject had not been altogether abrogated. Just as some of the terminology of earlier statutes had been used again in the new, so it was feared by a few that previous habits of thought would continue to prevail among prosecutors and judges who were destined to enforce it. In the very nature of its position as something new confronting an already long-established legal system, the Press Law, like a bird before a snake, would eventually be swallowed and digested at the latter's pleasure. As one deputy remarked to his colleagues in the parliamentary debates:

> Whatever the special articles you may vote, the *droit commun*, will not be the less applied whenever it is in the interest of the repressive authorities to use it. . . . Whatever the general provisions outlined [in the Press Law], they will be an addition, a superposition, and will not take the *droit commun* off the journalist's neck. The Press will be the unhappy beneficiary of this accumulation.[24]

From today's vantage point we can see that this prophecy of an "accumulation" has been borne out in still another way than that suggested by Deputy Gatineau. It is not only the prosecutors and judges who have brought old interpretations and meanings to the application of the Press Law; it is also that new legislation has been added to supplement the apparent deficiencies of the work of 1881. As early as 1893, new provisions were added to deal specifically with the problem of "anarchist propaganda." These additions marked the beginning of a turning away from jury trials wherever a publication appeared to have been put forth in furtherance of an anarchist thesis. Authors of such ideas were thenceforth to be sent before the *tribunaux correctionnels* both to minimize publicity for their cause and to assure summariness of decision.[25] The new statute also provided that all tribunals and courts could, at their own discretion, forbid the publication, in part or altogether, of the pleas and cross-examinations, insofar as such publication might "represent a danger for public order."

In addition, the so-called *lois scélérates* against anarchism contained one other change which the legislators of 1881 had originally refused to incorporate in the Press Law. It provided that incitement to the commission of the crimes and offenses enumerated in Chapter Four of the Press Law could be found to lie in an "apology" for a specific crime already committed. Thus, within fourteen years of the passage of the Press Law in its original form, legislative modifications had already begun to broaden its reach and facilitate the prosecution's task.[26]

The next important extensions of statutory control came after World War I. In 1920 the "horizon blue" Chamber passed a law forbidding all "propaganda" in favor of contraception or against a high birth rate. The restriction applied equally to any privately undertaken description of contraceptive techniques and devices. The desire of the deputies to see the demographic ravages of the War repaired was obvious enough. But in a country where the birth rate had for more than a century been among the lowest in Europe, the state of mind that could attribute such power to words is particularly striking.

The tensions of the thirties imposed further statutory restrictions. The growth of proto-fascist groups, the renascence of right-wing vindictiveness, such as that represented by Maurras and the *Action francaise*, fear of German rearmament and intentions, and the general inability of the parliamentary system to meet depression and social needs effectively, all led in default of social policy to new attempts to make repressive statutes do the work of maintaining order. Every year after 1935 was marked by one or more new laws and decrees restricting speech and press. By 1940 the Government was in a position to punish the expression of almost any idea or language it chose.[27] As one notable example, by the Law of July 11, 1938—Organization of the Nation in Time of War—reinforced by a decree-law of May 24, 1938, and later another one of July 29, 1939, the Government was enabled to rewrite those sections of the Penal Code dealing with treason, and to draw up restrictions on "secessionist propaganda" aimed at the secessionist movement then active in Brittany. And these provisions were to find use a generation later in the Algerian crisis.

Further modifications of the press laws took place after the War, most of them aimed at incorporating the prewar decree-laws into an ordered whole. The Ordinance of May 6, 1944, in particular laid to rest what had once been the key element of the procedures by the legislators of 1881—trial by jury. The new provisions established primary jurisdiction with the *tribunal correctionnel* for the whole range of offenses defined in the Press Law, except major crimes or felonies under the heading of Article 23. A modification which had thus been first applied to anarchists alone in 1894 became standard for virtually all who were likely to be charged under the Press Law. Whether the shift really meant a triumph for the forces of repression, however, is open to question. Trial by jury did not invariably produce a court favorable to the defendant—witness the trial of Emile Zola on account of his famous *J'Accuse!*[28] The abandonment of the jury probably reflected a discovery which the Third Republic was to make even more painfully in political life than legal, that no particular group or Frenchmen could be taken to stand for any other group, much less the People. Like the nation itself, the court system needed a certain unity that was not spontaneously produced anywhere by society itself.

Brief as its history proved to be, the Fourth Republic also left other statutory marks on freedom of expression. Two are especially worth noting, one because it reestablished a form of statutory censorship, if but advisory in nature, and the other because of its extension of police powers under certain conditions.

The first took shape with the Law of July 16, 1949, concerning juvenile publications. Its purpose is to exclude from all publications for children and adolescents

> any illustration, story, chronicle, title, or insertion which presents in a favorable light banditry, lying, theft, laziness, cowardice, hate, debauchery, or any act defined as a crime or delict or of such a nature as to demoralize children or young people, or (through a qualification made by the law of November 29, 1953) to inspire or uphold ethnic prejudices.

Beyond providing criminal sanctions, however, the new law also established a special commission attached to the Ministry of Justice "to oversee and control" publications for young people, requiring in effect that every publishing house producing magazines for juveniles do essentially the same by setting up an editorial committee within its own administration specifically responsible for supervision of the materials used. A 1958 ordinance added to this law a prohibition of the sale to any youth eighteen years or younger of

> all publications of whatever nature that present a threat to young people by reason of their licentious or pornographic character, or the place they give to crime.

Though acting in an advisory capacity, these commissions and editorial committees nevertheless represent a form of censorship behind which lies the threat of criminal liability. And in these matters, the spirit is more significant than the form.[29]

The second important statutory legacy of the Fourth Republic concerning free speech appears in the Law of April 3, 1955, Article II of which confers on prefects the power to search private premises day and night and to "prescribe all measures for assuring control of the press and of all publications of whatever kind . . ." during any period declared to be a "state of emergency" (*état d'urgence*) by parliament. Under pressure from both Algerian nationalists and rebellious army officers, the Fifth Republic early found ample occasion for using this provision.

Even without detailed description of other regulatory legislation, the historical trend towards extension of controls of speech and press is evident. Successive generations of legislators have never shown themselves satisfied with the work of 1881; and more than a few Frenchmen apparently share at least the last element of an opinion attributed to Mussolini, that France is a nation in constant danger of being ruined by "alcohol, syphillis, and journalism."

Indeed, distaste for the press was even more characteristic of de Gaulle's presidency than it was for the preceding one, as the joining of an official concern for national morale and public morals became more evident during his decade than it had in the previous eight. Under the Fourth Republic Premier Mendès-France had hoped to encourage the consumption of more milk and less alcohol. His government lasted seven and one-half months. But President de Gaulle lasted ten years while guarding morals all the way from the décolletage of lady guests at the presidential palace to new novels on the shelves of the small bookseller. This new wave of control required virtually no new legislation, however, and certainly none of a radically new kind, than that which the Fifth Republic found when it first appeared on stage. And though it is obviously incorrect to say that the bonapartist mentality which first developed the machinery of police control is still dominant, there is evidently enough latent fear of public spontaneity left in the nooks and crannies of the minds of most middle-class Frenchmen to make official harassment of speech and press always possible, if seldom altogether effective.

The matter of effectiveness leads us to ask whether such harassment is in fact wholly resented, even by those who feel it directly. Complaints about the authoritarianism of the Fifth Republic have long been rife in the intellectual and publishing worlds. More lawsuits involving freedom of speech and press, and publicity about them, have been noted since 1958 than before. One cannot help feeling, however, that resistance to enforcement of the political vision of those in power is not regarded by those who resist as a tiresome and peripheral activity drawing them away from the real business of their lives. On the contrary, it often seems to constitute the real heart of that business, because those who joust with the minions of the regime thereby act out political roles consecrated by a centuries-old perspective of French political culture.[30]

It is not simply a matter of defending certain *droits acquis*, although of course every publisher has a strong financial interest in the works he publishes. More important is the principle involved, which is the citizen's right to take an irresponsible position in the face of the State's tutelage. The citizen's relations with the State are defined in the public temples, and for those whose business is the dissemination of ideas, the rituals to which they have become devoted by usage are those of the Press Law and its amendments, while the altar at which they sacrifice is the Bar, with the aid of the priests of the law. In such cases, authors do not see their works cut merely for the fun of it. But when authorities offer the occasion, they obviously feel they would be remiss in their duties to the nation and even to humanity itself, to say nothing of their own interests, if they failed to employ all the means which ancient legal forms can provide.

Litigation thus continues to be a valued avocation, especially where it concerns freedom of speech, because from the perspective of the moral order there is nothing in which the play of words does not have a major part. The inherent uncertainties of the Press Law and the notions of order inevitably accompanying any of its applications offer a field where, indeed, a proper Frenchman can hardly refuse battle. He will accept not only because the meaning of the symbols by which he lives is at stake but also because the interpretation of press laws to specific cases is necessarily a subjective matter. Litigation thus offers a kind of confrontation with authority which is at once personal and universal: it satisfies an ultimate need of the French citizen by allowing him to regard both the commands of government and his own responses as questions of will in which humanity hangs in the balance. And since administrative law lays the burden of maintaining the immediate physical order on public authorities, the private citizen is left free to make public his own view with minimal concern for self-policing. While he may well regard obedience to authority for the sake of his own material interests to be prudent, he is implicitly freed from seeing the laws from which he draws private advantage as touchstones of justice. On the contrary, he will tend to look at the claims of existing authorities as expressing someone else's convenience; and since by definition mere convenience must fail to correspond to any ideal of justice, he will not only feel free to withhold support as soon as his own convenience permits, he will feel under obligation to attack.

The respective claims of public order and personal liberties are thus destined in France never to live even in a theoretical symbiosis, nor even to find a rough boundary set for them by statute. It is almost as if both Radicals and Opportunists, each their own way, had understood this in 1881, the Radicals by insisting that ideas could only be brought before the bar of public opinion, the Opportunists by insisting that only the "tutelary hand of the State" could protect the public from itself. Since neither group could express its views through new institutions, successive events reacted with old ones to produce legal processes that today seem to reflect a deeper sense of the French experience. Perhaps it was awareness of such a possibility that led the deputy, Cunéo d'Ornano, to remark in the course of the parliamentary debate on the Press Law that "where freedom of speech is concerned, I think everything depends on who the judge is."[31]

It was perhaps a pretty obvious thing to say, but in the light of the history of the development of legal procedures since 1881, one cannot help thinking it an extraordinarily appropriate one all the same. But its very aptness raises an awkward question for French judges. For if the public order must be the creation of a conscious act of political will to reflect even the formal attributes of justice, what business have the courts to participate according to their own professional lights in the making of the rules which help to define this order?

At first glance, this question should be especially bothersome for the administrative courts because they operate on the basis of procedures and judgments more clearly derived from their own peculiar perceptions and experiences than do the ordinary courts, which are ostensibly limited to the strict application of statutory law. We have indeed already seen the French response to this problem: since the public order has two elements, the one physical and the other moral, it is the task of administrative law alone to see that the former is adequately protected, if possible without prejudice to the rules of the latter. Yet in this age of incessant disorders, the "tutelary hand of the State" has increasingly expressed itself through police powers, and police powers have inevitably been expanded against public liberties. Immediately utility and expedience, as seen in the light of *la tutelle*, have come increasingly to encroach on the realm of the moral order itself. And a critical reflection of this encroachment has been the growing number and complexity of conflicts of jurisdiction between the two court systems, each concerned with its own perceptions of the public order. So I now turn to some particular examples of these conflicts, in order to show how they illustrate the sense of a deeper tension between what "right permits and interest demands." For it is in this feeling that French civic spirit has one of its clearest manifestations.

)

CHAPTER THREE

Jurisdictional Conflicts

The very considerations which judges most rarely mention,
and always with an apology, are the secret root from which
the law draws all the juices of life. I mean, of course, considerations of what is expedient for the community concerned.

Oliver Wendell Holmes, Jr., *The Common Law*

That everything should depend on who the judge is, of course,
is the kind of conclusion which suits the temper of modern
legal realism. Without the benefit of much philosophy, prac-
ticing lawyers have always recognized the advantage of familiarity with the demeanor and outlook of the judges who hear
their clients' cases. But in France "who the judge is" has a
special significance having only secondarily to do with the personal
disposition of individual members of the bench. Before analyzing
psychologies we must analyze procedures; the question is, before
which kind of judge—administrative or ordinary—will a case be
heard? On the answer to this question will depend very different
means of action and consequences.

The extension of administration into the realm of the law of
free speech is a striking example of the growth of law by means
other than the processes of statutory amendment because, as I
have shown, the legislators of 1881 gave little thought to such
administrative acts of censorship, except to condemn them
implicitly. They appeared to think that the principle of personal
liability would alone suffice for the maintenance of public order.
But the history of the Third Republic was to show otherwise,
and to bring about more than the legislative changes outlined

in the preceding chapter. Wars, depressions, internal strife—all were to elicit governmental responses built on the firm foundation of an administrative mode of thought long familiar in French politics both in thought and practice.

Although the essential ideas went back into the Old Regime, and beyond, and were to find some legislative reflection during the Revolution, public administration as the principal agent of public order was really perfected under the First Empire. The term "police state" is perhaps a bit harsh in the light of modern contemporary associations with the term, but the germ was and still is clearly there. The Ministry of the Interior in Paris was the core of the Napoleonic administration, and its means of control extended into the country through the centrally recruited and trained prefects, who were deployed out into the country as the most important link in the chain of central direction. Their primary local responsibility was to see to the maintenance of order in their respective districts. Under Bonaparte the prefects developed into bishops of a secular order, with many of the same kind of political, administrative, and even some of the judicial powers which their diocesian counterparts had held centuries previously. And for all the constitutional and political changes of the nineteenth and twentieth centuries, the prefects and the Ministry of the Interior are still awaiting a revolution to depose them.[1]

We shall thus hardly be surprised to find that the prefects' concern for public order was not much modified by the Press Law. Whether it was by acting through their own discretionary powers by bringing potentially illegal activities to the attention of the public prosecutor of their districts, directing their sections of the *gendarmerie nationale*, advising mayors, or acting as channels of important political and economic information between the *départements*, the Ministry in Paris, the prefects have always played a key role in the policing and politics of France.[2] And though the National Assembly of 1884, acting under something of the same kind of inspiration as the legislators responsible for the Press Law, passed the Law of Municipal Organization in 1884 in order to encourage a degree of local initiative and to allow locally elected officials to share responsi-

bility for the exercise of the police powers once held by prefects alone, it was still careful to make clear that mayors were
in the last analysis subordinate, if not altogether dependent,
on the prefects.[3]

It was, nevertheless, through this slender concession to municipal authorities that the Council of State was able to enter the
realm of judicial review of administrative acts bearing on public
order, a legal challenge to local officials being more discreet
than one to agents of the central government. For the Council,
once Bonaparte's key institution for assuring central control and
direction of the administrative system, was to evolve toward
becoming a relatively independent judicial agency whose history
has encouraged its present membership to think of themselves
as an elite with special responsibilities for guarding constitutional
coherence and civil liberties. From having been a tool of the
tyrant for the purposes of administrative efficiency, the Council
of State became minister to a liberal regime by means of
developing limits on administrative practices according to its
own reflection of the needs of modern democracy. If the
evolution of these practices has been somewhat uncertain and
occasionally even tortuous, it is no doubt because both events
and republican theory have made discretion the better part of
valor for French judges.

The difficulties they face stem from an ambivalence characteristic of modern democratic thought that is particularly sharp
in France. On the one hand, democracy is a way of organizing
public power. This organization is considered legitimate in the
measure that it creates and maintains citizenship, a status in
which each individual is given an opportunity to quit his un-
reflective tendency to serve himself exclusively by becoming a
member of a moral community. On the other hand, democracy
is also a form of administration which acts to protect persons,
properties, and established interests by means of redress against
the arbitrary exercise of power, no matter how beneficial to the
public this exercise may in any given case seem to be. It is on the
basis of conflicts arising from these two aspects of democracy
that the Council of State has built its reputation as balancer
of public will and private interests.

But as I was saying, no legislator in 1881 seemed to be aware that the needs of public order would sooner or later result in the intervention of administrative officials in the exercise of free speech. As guardian and mentor of civic—as distinct from property—rights, the first flowering of the Council of State came with the personnel issues raised by the separation of Church and State. The consequences of the *loi Combe* for teachers in France's primary and secondary public schools were enormous. Entering into the political spirit which had originally motivated the separation, many zealous public school administrators began to weed out of their teaching staffs those whom they suspected of being tainted by clerical and sometimes only merely orthodox Catholic sentiments. Because the victims of this campaign of secular purification were civil servants, it became a matter for the Council of State to define the nature of their contractual relationships with the State. This the Council did in a series of decisions dating from 1906 to the beginning of the First World War. Given the spirit and political forces of the time, its judges acted both with some courage and success in protecting the claims of private conscience among state employees. The fact that specific contract rights were at stake no doubt facilitated its task. But the material elements of the question aside, the Council showed a capacity to take a stand for a conception of human rights distinct from that urged by immediate legislative majorities. And administrative officials with police responsibilities were at least reminded that their hierarchic superiors were not the last word on what the law said.

But protecting the civil servant's right to hold private convictions is one thing, protecting a citizen's right to speak in public another. In the former matter the Council of State was really helping to define the limits of a legislative act which was aimed exclusively at the administration itself. Where free speech is concerned, things have been much more complicated. The Catholic school teacher was found to have a right to hold both his private religious belief and his public job so long as the two were not mixed. Questions of the nature of the public order did not have to be faced directly. When a man asks, however, not simply the right to hold his own convictions in private, but wants to make them public in order to convert other people to his point of view, every aspect of the public order is potentially in question.

The distinctions between the *régime répressif* and the *régime préventif* sound clear enough in theory, and very often they will be so in practice as well. And yet for all reasonableness of these distinctions, the two court systems do sometimes find themselves in jurisdictional conflict, and the consequences of such conflict are more likely to give joy to those who would suppress free speech than to those who love it. How this may come about and what the result can be is best illustrated, I think, by the story of four cases. One of these dates from 1935, the others from 1960, 1961, and 1962 respectively, and while I cannot argue their relative importance in itself, they do nevertheless typify conflicts of the two jurisdictions, and some of the consequences which may flow therefrom.

These dates are indicative of the same kind of evolution in the realm of legal procedures as we have already seen in the preceding outline of statutory developments during the twentieth century: more rules and greater complexities. Before World War I there were very few complaints about prior restraints resulting from police action. The leading case in this realm, *de Lajudre v. Pomarède et al*, was disposed of handily by the Court of Cassation in 1914 in favor of the jurisdiction of the ordinary courts and, consequently, against any administrative prior restraint. The fact that the Court of Cassation had to quash the judgment of a court of appeals was, perhaps, prophetic of troubles to come, however. At issue was a police action in the form of destruction of political posters put up in the Herault district. In 1899, the prefect of that *département* had made a blanket decree against the use of political posters anywhere within his jurisdiction, and in 1909 police officer Pomarède and his agents had destroyed certain posters put up by de Lajudre. The latter brought suit against the police in the civil courts for compensation of the financial loss he had suffered, and on appeal from the trial court, the Court of Appeals at Montpellier refused jurisdiction saying, on the point of law, that the police officers were not legally bound to read the orders of their superior with a lawyer's eye, and that so far as the validity of the prefectoral order itself was concerned, only the administrative courts could properly determine the issue. Here is the response of the Court of Cassation:

> Whereas the acts for which the [police officers] are reproached are . . . forbidden by the law; they therefore do not deal with a matter within the realm of administration, and are thus in effect only personal and arbitrary acts . . . constituting injury to private property. Since a prefectoral order can neither cover nor justify them, it is the duty of the ordinary courts to deal with them. . . .
>
> Whereas the law of July 29, 1881, has [created] absolute liberty of posting for political as well as other forms of bills . . . the Court of Appeals, in deciding otherwise [than according to this rule] did thereby make a false application of the principle of the separation of powers, misread its own competence, and violated the provisions of the law. . . .[5]

Notice how simple the matter of jurisdictions seemed in 1914: when administrative acts haven't a legal leg to stand on, they have no status to justify their being dealt with as administrative acts at all. Hence the ordinary courts have jurisdiction to dispose of the claims involved as though they were claims arising from private parties. Obvious illegality of administrative behavior immediately places litigation into the hands of the ordinary courts, which are obligated to read the relevant statutes alone. Obvious administrative wrong decides the question of jurisdiction, and the only question left is what the State's agents may have to pay in damages.

World War I marked the great breach in this simple procedural perspective. The formal means of this breaching came with the legislative declaration of a state of seige in the northern regions where the fighting took place, with the consequent disposition of all legal matters in military courts. For obvious reasons these military courts were far less interested in justice than they were in effective policing, less interested in punishment and

civil claims than in prior restraint. The jurisprudential consequences of this state of affairs, not inevitable perhaps, but
natural enough, turned out to be elaboration of new rules
extending the scope of police action. In the terminology of
administrative lawyers this elaboration has become identified
and defined as a theory of *circonstances exceptionnelles* (exceptional circumstances), and its thrust has been, of course, to
give form to the idea of clear and present danger.[6]

As is implicitly suggested by the Council of State in the
Benjamin case, a judicial finding of exceptional circumstances
will enlarge the scope for prior restraint. But in so doing it will
also inevitably raise the question of the proper jurisdiction to
hear the issues and the kind of perspective from which the issues
will be seen and dealt with. Exceptional circumstances mean
we are no longer in the realm of individual but rather in that of
relative social wrong.

But from the point of view of the complainant, they may
mean his being in a realm of absolute confusion and frustration.
The difficulty is compounded by the fact that responsibility
for the determination of exceptional circumstances, a finding
absolutely central to the ways and means of disposing of the
claims involved, will ultimately fall, if the plaintiff pushes hard
enough, on a special court called the *Tribunal des conflits*,
which does nothing else than decide jurisdictional conflicts
between the two court systems, but whose judgments on this
very matter have been often found, in the words of a recent
puzzled *commissaire du gouvernement*, to reflect *un byzantisme
excessif*.[7] But we do not need to take an expert's word for it;
let the reader judge for himself in the following instances.

The first case again involves *Action française*, both as a movement and as a newspaper. The circumstances are of critical importance because they suggest the length to which elements of
the French legal system have at times been willing to go to draw
the line between proper and improper administrative acts.

The events giving rise to this particular case occurred on the
morning of February 7, 1934—very early in the morning in fact.
By seven o'clock identical messages from the Paris Prefect of
Police had been phoned to every police station in Paris and the

Seine district, forbidding the display and sale of all copies of that day's issue of Maurras' newspaper within the entire *département*. A sweeping and drastic order, it was effectively carried out because all newspaper dealers in the public thoroughfares throughout the region had periodically reviewable police licenses to do business, and they were only too ready to cooperate with the police in order to protect their concessions.

Maurras and his codirectors were understandably angry. Readership of *Action française* had been increasing steadily over the past few years, and nowhere faster than in the Paris region. As the weaknesses of the Third Republic, both structural and personal, became increasingly evident, antidemocratic, anti-parliamentary invective became correspondingly more popular. And in the February 7 issue of *Action française* Maurras had outdone himself in brilliant and bitter denunciations of the regime. From his point of view, indeed, he had had especially good material to work with.[8]

This material had been spectacularly produced by the events of the preceding day. On February 6, 1934, the unfortunate National Assembly had been trapped in the *Palais Bourbon* for the better part of the afternoon and evening by angry mobs, demanding a wide variety of things, but all apparently agreeing that the existing government had outlived its usefulness. More important in Maurras' view, these riots had been accompanied by some bloodshed, which Maurras was only too happy to blame on the Daladier Government and on its Socialist Minister of the Interior, Eugene Frot. It was this particular message *Action française* carried on the morning of February 7, and which the Prefect of Police had tried to suppress by ordering immediate seizure.

Never lacking competent legal advice in his lifelong struggle against the Republic, Maurras brought suit against the Prefect of Police in person in a civil court at Versailles, demanding punitive damages for the banning of the newspaper on February 7. In response, Bonnefoy-Sibour denied the jurisdiction of the court at Versailles to hear the case on its merits, arguing that according to the basic republican theory of the separation of powers no challenge to administrative acts could originate in the regular courts. So a conflict of jurisdictions between regular and administrative courts was opened up. How was it to be decided?

In Maurras' view, it could be settled only in favor of the regular court where he had begun suit. His claim was based on a rule of jurisprudence which had first been made clear in 1873. According to this rule, administrative acts doing harm to private interests might be categorized in either one of two ways. Either the general functioning of the administrative service itself might be at fault, in which case this *faute de service* led to the jurisdiction of the administrative courts which alone were competent to decide the case on its merits; or the injury might have arisen from the *faute personnel* of some particular State agent, in which case the extent of his liability was a private matter to be determined by the regular courts. In bringing suit for punitive damages against Bonnefoy-Sibour, Maurras gave audacious litigious expression to his political conviction: the accusation of a *faute personnelle* against the Prefect was intended to provide but further proof of the corruption of a parliamentary system which appointed public officials who routinely acted in the service of their political friends (i.e., Daladier and Frot) rather than in the service of the nation.

The Prefect's refusal to accept the writ of the Versailles court—in this instance that of a *juge de paix*—meant that the case could not be heard on its merits until the issue of jurisdiction had been settled. In French terminology the Prefect of Police had done what all other prefects have a right to do—*élever le conflit*—such conflicts of jurisdiction to be decided by the *Tribunal des conflits*.[9]

The *Tribunal des conflits* handed down its decision in the case of *Action Francais v. Bonnefoy-Sibour* on April 8, 1935. The civil court at Versailles could properly hear and judge the claim on its merits, it said, but if damages were awarded they would have to be laid against the State itself and not against Bonnefoy-Sibour personally. The *Tribunal* decided, in short, that the distinction between *faute de service* and *faute personnelle* was not the appropriate principle in the case, and even that the normal view of the separation of powers was not determinative, because this time the State itself was to be held answerable for its acts in an ordinary court.

The legal basis of this extraordinary decision is to be found in the term *voie de fait*, which may be loosely translated as an "act of violence," or as "taking the law into one's own hands." The *Tribunal des conflits* found that the Prefect of Police had engaged the State in just such an act, and that the State's responsibility for any claims resulting therefrom was consequently absolute, and not to be legally mitigated by any considerations arising from the maintenance of public order. The theory of the *voie de fait* goes way back into the nineteenth century. But it had always been thought to apply exclusively to unlawful damage to private property rights alone. Here in 1935, the *Tribunal des conflits* at last extended the principle to cover injury to a fundamental civic right as defined by the Press Law of 1881. In its simplest terms the theory says that the State *qua* State cannot under any circumstances *will* acts of violence against private citizens. When it does do them in fact, it can no longer claim the public interest as a reason and it may therefore be held to answer for them in the regular courts just as if it were itself a private citizen.

We have here the most dramatic, although hardly the most useful, of weapons available in French law for the protection of citizens' rights against administrative acts. Its underlying motive is to insist that even under the strongest demands of expedience public authorities are bound to legal requirements and that the State cannot properly be imputed with the will to break the bond. But its utility from the private citizen's point of view is severely limited by the maneuvers, delays, and expenses imposed by the necessity of seeking solution of the jurisdictional conflict through the *Tribunal des conflits* in which, incidentally, the Minister of Justice, who will clearly have a political interest in certain cases, may be in a position to cast the deciding vote.[10]

Let us turn now to our second case involving potential conflict of the *régime répressif* and the *régime préventif*. The setting this time is more recent; the circumstances of this case arose in the first insurrection of the European settlers in Algiers against the policy of self-determination for the territory of Algeria. The idea of self-determination had first been hinted at by President de Gaulle in December 1959. Since the Europeans in Algeria generally considered the very idea to be a betrayal, some of them took the time-honored manner of protesting by going to the barricades. These were set up in the public square before the government house in Algiers in January, 1960. A small band of Europeans in Algiers swore to remain in possession, by force of arms if need be, until they had received categorical assurances from Paris that Algeria would remain forever under French sovereignty.

Because the French Army showed a great reluctance to use force against a group of people with whom at least many of its professionals tended to sympathize, the barricades remained in place a week. When they finally did come down, some ten of the insurrectionists were arrested, along with one Alain de Sérigny, editor and publisher of the city's major newspaper, *L'Echo d'Alger*. The ensuing trial eventually became the longest in modern French history, lasting from November 1960 until March 1961.

The charge against de Sérigny in particular was that his editorials had incited the Europeans of Algiers to undertake the insurrection. He was therefore prosecuted under Article 23 of the Press Law, as an accomplice to a crime which he had himself publicly recommended. His defense, undertaken by Maîtres Isorni and de Richemond, was based largely on the jurisdictional issue. Counsel argued that de Sérigny could not be held criminally liable for provocation because *l'Echo d'Alger* had in fact been under military censorship throughout the entire period the articles in question were being published. Censorship, defense counsel argued, precluded de Sérigny's liability, since the military authorities were in a position to delete any materials they believed to be provocative or disturbing to the public order. Legally speaking, the materials actually published in *l'Echo d'Alger* received, so it was argued, the State's implicit approval. The editor could therefore not be held liable for any offenses which the pages of his newspaper might conceivably have contained.

The prosecution's rebuttal is worth reproducing in part for the light it throws on a characteristically French theory of the relationship between the administrative law and justice. Admitting that the brief put forward in de Sérigny's behalf appeared to have "considerable weight and the favor of the general public" with it, the State's attorney nevertheless found that if the matter were put in its proper legal framework the answer would become clear. This framework he proceeded to describe as follows:

> Censorship and police seizure are measures that fall within the realm of the public powers. But in the absence of seizure, the visa of censorship can have no effect on the legality of the published text, for which the author or other responsible persons may always be held liable. Whether censored or not, the publisher remains responsible for what is published. The author may argue his good faith. Censorship may be used as an attentuating circumstance but nothing more . . . . The element of intention may be eliminated and liability may become more restricted. But the latter nevertheless continues insofar as the headlines and the setting up of the pages are concerned. . . . In any case, administrative control is directed toward the maintenance of public order. The kind of control provided by the ordinary courts is altogether different. The prosecution must oversee with respect to legality to assure itself that laws are not being transgressed. Public order is not its business. Administrators and judges have each their own realm of action; but these realms are never joined, nor can the one exclude the other. It is not the function of the police or the censor to judge.[11]

As to Counsel's further argument that liability would have to be shown for each of the incriminating texts taken individually, the prosecutor maintained rather that they must be taken as a whole for it was only in the light of their general tendency and progression that their truly provocative effect could be seen.

We mustn't forget that [the defendant] was an influential member of the City and of the Press, and was aware of his power. For the local population his newspaper was both Bible and breviary.

In his reply by way of summation, defense counsel Isorni simply declared the prosecutor's statement of the relationship between censorship and liability to be an "imposture." And turning toward the journalists in the courtroom he added:

I am defending here the liberty of each one of you, and though there may be some who regret that the occasion of this defense has to be de Sérigny's trial, this is nevertheless the occasion.

The court acquitted de Sérigny, along with twelve of his co-defendants. This result, however, cannot be read as a categorical rejection of the prosecutor's theory of the relationship of the *régime répressif* and the *régime préventif*. The *procès des barricades* was manifestly a political trial through and through, and the motives of the court seem to have been regarded by all concerned as being more in keeping with this spirit than the juridical.

The third case is more recent yet. It concerns the well-known author Alfred Fabre-Luce and a book of his published in late 1962. The date is important because the last third of 1962 had been a bad time, legally speaking, for President de Gaulle. In October alone the Constitutional Council had declared his proposal for a referendum to pass a bill for popular election of the President unconstitutional, the Council of State had declared illegal the special Court of Military Justice which he had established to try members of the *Organisation de l'Armée Sécrète* and all its judgments null and void, and the Cabinet had been overthrown by the first successful motion of censure in the Fifth Republic's history. On top of these reversals came Fabre-Luce's book *Haute Cour* in the middle of December.

The tenor of the work is indicated by its title. President de Gaulle's own Constitution of 1958 had provided procedures for the establishment of a High Court of Justice (*Haute Cour*). The sole function of this court should the matter ever arise, is to try the President of the Republic on an indictment of high treason offered by Parliament. *Haute Cour* recounted such an hypothetical trial, with President de Gaulle himself as defendant.

The book reached booksellers' shelves on December 16. On December 19, 1962, all copies of *Haute Cour* were seized by the police in all the bookstores in France. The prefects' orders were issued according to instructions sent them from the Minister of the Interior. The order averred danger to public order as the motive and referred to Article 16 of the Constitution of 1958 as its legal basis.

In January 1963, Fabre-Luce's publisher, *Editions* Julliard, wrote to the Prime Minister, asking an explanation for the seizure. In his reply, M. Pompidou, the newly reinstated prime minister, referred not to any immediate danger to the public order but rather to an offense against the "person of the President under Article 26 of the Press Law and/or Article 222 of the Criminal Code." He explained the matter this way:

> In a liberal regime in which the President plays an essential role in orienting general policy, it is normal that this policy and, of course, the acts of the President be the object of debate and criticism. . . . But for the very honor of France, it is necessary that these criticisms, vehement as they may be and however determined the opposition may be, shall fall within certain limits with regard not to policy but to the person of the Head of State. Every Frenchman who has respect for himself, precisely because he does so, feels that he must respect the one whom the national will has put at the head of the country, and never more so than when this Frenchman does not approve of the Government's policy.
>
> The work in question appears to me even in its very theme offensive to the person of the Head of State.

The prime minister's argument permitted M. Fabre-Luce, in an open letter published by *le Monde*, to point out the apparent contradiction of juridical motives now involved:

You write that the public powers were constrained to "seize and prosecute." I don't know where the constraint you mention comes from. It certainly does not arise from any evidence of a delict. Indeed, although the Minister of the Interior did request on December 20 that the Minister of Justice lay an indictment for offense to the Head of State, neither my publisher nor myself have received notice of such a charge.

During these two months of reflection the Minister of Justice must have felt some scruples. He has perhaps discovered that *Haute Cour* is essentially a literary work, written with moderation, and a great deal more respectful toward the Head of State than many other writings touching on the same subject, which have neither been seized nor prosecuted . . .

Even if at the end of his meditations the Minister of Justice tardily attributes to me an intent to offend the Head of State, an intent I did not have, it would nevertheless be true that such an indictment cannot by itself justify a seizure undertaken before a court judgment has been handed down. Now in your letter of January 17 you raise no other complaint, and do not on your own account take up that concern for public order invoked by the Prefect of Police to justify the seizure.

Even if on this point you decide—after receiving this letter—to take a new position, it would not change the fact that public safety may not be validly invoked in this instance in such terms as those cited by the Prefect in his decision of December 20. His text, on that date, was null and void. Furthermore, it was aimed at a subversive movement which I specifically condemned in the seized work.

For these reasons I am today requesting legal redress for "*exces de pouvoir*" on the part of the Prefect of Police from the Paris Administrative Tribunal.[12]

In fact, after a good deal more "meditation" prosecution against the author was finally brought. M. Fabre-Luce lost this criminal case in a decision rendered December 20, 1963.

He likewise lost an appeal to the Paris Court of Appeals. So not only had *Haute Cour* been seized administratively allegedly for reasons of public order, but this seizure was later confirmed, though it was not justified, by a criminal proceeding against its author on the charge of insult to the Chief of State. In commenting on this condemnation in a later work, M. Fabre-Luce remarked:

> In my characterizations of the President, [the judges] reproached me for using the names of animals. The prosecution's indictment referred notably to a certain "mammoth" who appeared on one of my pages. I was taken by surprise. I had always thought this animal . . . had left a good name for itself. Fortunately for me, the court let the mammoth go by, but another animal was unable to pass the barrier. Which one? For nothing on earth will I reveal which. I am, and intend to remain, a citizen who respects the principle of *res judicata*. I feel, however, a certain difficulty in grasping my exact duty. I should like to have a list of animals one is forbidden to mention. The presiding judge, unfortunately, did not give me one.[13]

As to the case brought by Fabre-Luce and *Editions* Julliard against the Prefect of Police for the seizure of *Haute-Cour* on December 20, 1962, the plaintiffs undertook a new tack on July 12, 1963. Desisting in the earlier action for annullment of the original seizure they instead requested the release of the volumes seized, on the ground that whatever the legal status of the prefectoral order of seizure as of December 20, 1962, the alleged state of emergency (*état d'urgence*) which might conceivably have been held to exist at that time, and which might therefore have given a color of legality to the original seizure, was now certainly terminated by law as of May 31, 1963, and that as a consequence the seized books must be returned to their rightful owners. Here again the Prefect of Police, acting on orders from the Minister of the Interior, demurred, claiming that no restitution could properly be made so long as the criminal proceedings against Fabre-Luce for insult to the Chief of

State were still to be judged. All copies of the work were thus held by the police until the criminal courts completed their hearings and rendered final judgment against Fabre-Luce, ordering him and *Editions* Julliard to pay fines of $300 each, and the physical destruction of all copies. Three years later, however, the plaintiffs in the administrative action did receive some satisfaction: the Administrative Tribunal of Paris declared null and void the earlier refusal of the Prefect to restore the books to their rightful owners, and this decision was upheld by the Council of State on December 20, 1967, against an appeal by the Minister of the Interior. The basic legal argument leading to this result was that the actions and procedures in the criminal and administrative courts had no necessary connection with each other, each having to be decided on its own merits without reference to proceedings or judgments in courts of the other system. In short, justice and police powers, law and order, have each their own procedures, rules, and judgments.

Here again the principal recompense for author and publisher was moral, for although these decisions of the administrative courts in theory opened the way to requesting damages for the illegal seizure, what value could be put on the copies of a work which had already been ordered destroyed by the *Tribunal correctionnel*? Fabre-Luce and *Editions* Julliard may have had the pleasure of proving the government to be a bad policeman, but the final result nevertheless seems to reflect closely the moral of La Fontaine's fable of the lamb and the wolf.[14]

To these cases where the confusion of administrative and statutory authorities is so evident must be added one more which, historically inevitable as it may appear in retrospect, is no less bizarre. Here again the issue is prior restraint. But the powers involved are not this time exclusively police powers; that is, they are not police powers in origin even though they may be in effect. Though the source of the confusion of jurisdictions lay in the Press Law itself, the courts of both jurisdictions seem to have contributed their respective bits to the morass, so that there are some observers who believe that the way out will not be by way of legislative fiat alone. Rather, they say, since the judges got us into the mess, they will have to help get us out!

The statutory origin of the problem lies in two conflicting provisions. On the one hand, we have the prohibition of the first paragraph of Article 51 of the Press Law, limiting police seizure of any publication to four copies for the purpose of providing evidence in possible criminal proceedings. On the other, we have Article 30 of the *Code de procédure pénale* (prior to 1959, Article 10 of the *Code d'instruction criminelle*) which provides that in all instances where state security may be at stake, prefects can order the seizure of all instruments of the alleged threat as incriminating evidence, according, so says the second paragraph of Article 51 of the Press Law, to the *Code de procédure pénale*. In acting under Article 51 the prefects are fulfilling a function of what the French call the *police judiciaire*: they are in priniciple acting as agents of the criminal court system. But the very term *police judiciaire* suggests awkward jurisdictional problems. As agents of the ordinary courts the prefects' acts ought to come in principle under the review of the ordinary courts; but as administrative agents their acts are, according to the French theory of the separation of powers, subject only to review in the administrative courts. Yet the latter are not authorized to review application of Article 30 of the *Code proc. pén.*, because its uses concern only the operations of the criminal courts. Thus we have a loophole made to order for lovers of legal intricacies and defenders of police powers, but of fearful potential for freedom of speech.

The confusions inherent in these statutory provisions came to a practical head particularly during the war of Algerian independence. Successive ministers of the Interior took advantage of the loophole to have prefects order seizures of whole issues of certain newspapers and journals on the ground that they contained indictable material relating to state security, only to drop charges once the particularly touchy situation they really had had in mind was past. In this way prior restraint could be exercised without police officials' having to worry about a review of the facts in the Council of State according to the de-

manding principles set forth in the Benjamin case, or indeed any
court review at all.

The device worked for a surprising number of seizures. But
the civil liberties' lawyers were soon warmed enough to prepare
a number of different cases. While some of these emphasized the
jurisdiction of the ordinary courts, others emphasized that of
the administrative courts. Thus, though having at first been
loathe to deal with such matters, both jurisdictions finally took
them on, with the result that beginning in 1960 we have a number of decisions which proposed, as we should now suppose
likely, rather different solutions.

The Council of State first dealt broadly with the matter in the
Frampar case, which arose from an order of the Prefect of Algiers
commanding the seizure of all copies of the January 6 and 7,
1957, issues of the newspapers *Le Monde, France-Soir,* and *Paris-
Presse* on the pier in Algiers on the ostensible grounds that articles in these issues contained delictual materials affecting the
internal and external security of the State, and that it was necessary to seize the evidence as per Article 10 (now 30) of the Code
of Criminal Instruction for use in a subsequent indictment and
trial. The newspapers originally brought suit against this seizure
in the Administrative Tribunal in Algiers, which declared itself
incompetent because, to all appearances, the matter concerned
an exercise of the police acting, not as agents of administration,
but as agents of the criminal courts *(police judiciaire)* and therefore, by the doctrine of the separation of powers, outside of the
jurisdiction of the administrative courts. *France-Soir* appealed
against this decision to the Council of State, arguing that the
seizure was an illegal administrative act for which it was owed
damages. Thus on the question of jurisdiction, the Council of
State stated:

> It is obvious from the circumstances taken as a whole . . .
> that the object of the seizures was not to obtain evidence of
> the commission of crimes against the . . . security of the
> State for the purpose of bringing the authors before the
> courts for punishment, but to prevent the distribution in
> Algiers of certain materials contained in the issues of the

newspapers in question. Hence, despite the fact that the evidence was duly submitted to the prosecutor of the criminal court for his action, the seizures really had the character of administrative acts . . . and the plaintiffs were justified in asking for annulment of the decision by the Administrative Tribunal of Algiers that [wrongly] declared its own lack of jurisdiction. . . .

And on the merits of the issue itself, the Council went on to say:

> The evidence makes clear that in ordering the seizure of the newspapers in question the Prefect's intention was to forestall disturbances which he thought the distribution of certain articles in the newspapers . . . likely to provoke. But to attain this purpose he could have used powers which he properly held, had he believed himself so justified . . . Thus, as the plaintiff companies maintain, in passing up proper procedures in order to use that contained in Article 10 of the Code of Criminal Instruction, whose field of action is limited . . . to determining whether crimes against the . . . security of the State have been committed and bringing their authors to justice, the Prefect of Algiers committed *un excès de pouvoir*.[15]

That the simplicity of this juridical solution is merely apparent, however, becomes evident when we consider the same sort of instance from the perspective of the regular courts. Take, for example, the fate of the case of the newspaper *Libération*, a journal whose outlook was largely if in some sense independently Communist, and whose particular cause was favorable to Algerian independence. In December 1960, acting under orders from the Ministry of the Interior, all prefects in France seized all copies of two succeeding issues of *Libération* on the ostensible authority of Article 30 (formerly 10) of the Code of Criminal Instruction, and in Paris the Prefect of Police duly submitted four of these copies to the *parquet* for the preferment of charges against the publisher, editor, and author of certain articles. But the public prosecutor failed to see anything indictable in either issue and ordered the seized copies returned to the publisher. Since old newspapers do have certain uses in France, but are hardly saleable, the publisher brought *civil suit* under Article 1382 of the Civil Code against the Prefect of Police for compensation of his financial loss, which he claimed to be 50,000 francs ($10,000). And he asked at the same time that the public treasury be made liable for the Prefect's debt. In due course, the court of first instance found the Prefect was indeed civilly liable, although not for any copies which had actually been returned, and that his fault, though in some sense a personal one, was nevertheless not, as the lawyers say, detachable from his public functions; hence the public treasury was indeed liable. In brief, the State was ordered to pay 1,500 francs damages ($300).[16] Both the Prefect and the Treasury appealed, winning effective reversal of the lower court's order in the Paris Court of Appeals. At this point we enter the realm of confusion rampant.

The appeals' court reversed on the ground that the plaintiff publisher had brought action against the Prefect under the wrong heading. Article 1382 of the Civil Code might have been an appropriate vehicle for reparation, it said, if in fact what the Prefect had committed had really been equivalent to what the administrative courts call personal fault (*faute personnelle*). But, said the judges, how could his seizure have amounted to a personal fault when it was perfectly clear that the Government was at the time of the act engaged in a kind of two front police action, against dissident Moslems on the one hand and dissident Europeans on the other? The Prefect's act might not therefore be justifiable by all the fine points of the law, but in the light of the *unusual circumstances* it was certainly not an unreasonable one and thus could not be attributed to wrongdoing in the degree necessary to bring his personal civil liability into play. Granted that the State might be shown to be financially responsible for the plaintiff's loss under the right form of action, plaintiff's brief had not raised these other possibilities, and the court of appeals was by its own tradition forbidden to raise them. Case dismissed, with expenses on the plaintiff. We have here, in short, an ordinary court, accepting its own jurisdiction but refusing to settle the cause before it by reference to its own jurisprudence and the statutes by which it is presumably bound in order to apply instead a principle of administrative law—note the reference to "unusual circumstances"—which, by the separation of powers it ought presumably to ignore! We can only suppose that the last word has not yet been said.[18]

So the possibility of the "*triste cumul*" of which Representative Gatineau spoke when the Press Law was passed in 1881 has on occasion developed a scope which might well have taken even his breath away. Yet we perhaps ought not to judge the system in too harsh a light. We need to remember that the activity of public powers to repress and suppress freedom of speech by more or less legal means should not, in the last analysis, be taken in isolation from the cultural atmosphere which has given rise to it. At least since Tocqueville it has been a truism to note that the "tyranny of the majority" expresses itself far more generally than overt legal means do. In this respect, the greater elaboration of the French governmental means intended to control freedom of speech in comparison with the American reflects not only the greater sense of danger to the integrity of the nation and a greater legalism which, in earlier times distinguished all continental countries from America but, at least in France, an atmosphere congenial to the propagation of ideas.[19]

This atmosphere is reflected in part in the very existence of the two jurisdictions—*régime préventif* and *régime répressif.* The distinction between types of order inherent in them suggests an approach toward liberating speech from the spirit of the Blackstonian principle of criminal liability with its particular implications for self-censorship. By concentrating judicial review on elaborating the procedures and standards which authorities must adhere to in maintaining a physical order that is manifestly their primary responsibility, instead of emphasizing the motives and behavior of individual citizens, French legal procedures reflect a psychological expectation on the part of the speaker that the expression of his ideas shall not be restricted by fear of personal liability for failure to be silent as his contribution to the maintenance of the immediate physical public order.

The mere statement of such an expectation in itself is perhaps too abstract to make much differentiation between the social ideas of Frenchmen and Americans. But its importance lies not so much in its statement as in its implications. It is the legal reflection of a fundamental social fact, that Frenchmen tend to feel freer of public obligations to the "public thing" in a psychological sense. They do not in fact feel personally responsible either for the opinions of their group, or for maintaining any form of conventional wisdom because of the circumstances of the moment. The prices paid for this form of independence are a weakening of normal means by which civic spirit may express itself, on the one hand, and a degree of arrogance and exclusivity on the part of the State's agent, on the other.

The association between this personal sense of independence and the dual legal regimes, *préventif* and *répressif*, inevitably reflects a conception of authority which has important implications for human rights. By insisting on the limited, physical character of police action the system throws into sharp relief the sovereignly *moral* character of legislation, and thus emphasizes the abyss between the appearance of order and the reality of justice. This means in practice that the legitimacy of no French regime will stem from a capacity to maintain a mere outward appearance of harmony and prosperity. It will rather depend ultimately on its ability to propagate an ethical point of view. A regime which fails to make its own convictions clear, which merely reflects the pressures and interests of the time in a more or less empirical way, will not have the loyalty of the citizen, even when he tolerates it, or uses it to his personal advantage. Thus the old definition of the Frenchman as a man who wears his heart on the left and his wallet on the right has the sense of a basic feature of the legal system behind it.

The corresponding characteristic of the French political outlook is consequently a demand for an intuited ethical quality reflected in positive law. This demand requires of those who govern that they provide the basic assumptions about the place of humanity in the context of history from which deductions about public affairs may be drawn. To object that such assumptions cannot be provided in advance because to do so is to foreclose opportunities and occasions for advance and change essential to public liberty, progress and utility, is to raise the fundamental dilemma or paradox of French political life. To reject *a priori* conceptions of justice is to place humanity wholly in an historical or existential world, where only the most profound skepticism—"the rats don't ask where the ship is going," in Voltaire's words—or of the most profound faith—God looks after all His creatures to the best advantage of all—will do. It is precisely these two extremes which French attitudes characteristically reject, recognizing that such a rejection means that the strength of political views comes not from experimentation but from a collective will to believe and to act.

It is also clear that the practical nub of this outlook must lie in the operation of actual institutions. To say that collective will to believe is the only source of those conceptions of justice necessary to legitimize political authority is all very well so long as one does not have to identify the institutions which give voice to this will. But the moment such identification becomes necessary the real problem of modern French political life is upon us, because will personalizes politics by making it a matter of ideas, and hence of the men who hold and propagate them, rather than of social, economic, and historical interests and forces they might otherwise be seen as representing. Consequently, institutional arrangements are judged according to their capacity to produce men and ideas rather than men and ideas judged according to their manifestation of organizational competence.

The state's claim to legitimacy is therefore implicitly, if not explicitly, as broad and all-embracing as are the ethical notions which inform the whole of life itself. And hence all centers of ethical consciousness other than those of the state, whether individual or institutional, have finally but one place to go, and that is into one or another form of opposition to the powers-that-be.[20]

Since 1789 the idea of human rights in France has therefore sprung far more consistently in practice from the idea of opposition to the existing regime than from participation in it. The ironic but necessary application of Rousseau's theory of the general will in France has been that in serving one historical revolution it has come to serve the idea of permanent revolution as well. The citizen, in short, is more likely to develop his own moral identity in politics in ostensible conflict with those in office than in contributing to an extension of their logic.

Individual rights thus come into play in the form of absolutes, and the role of the courts in "protecting" them must necessarily be very small indeed. Whatever attempt there has been to say that individual rights and public needs may in specific instances be reconciled in France—and this attempt is really apparent only in the jurisprudence of the administrative courts—there are few to argue, as liberal American thinking would have it, that rights may be legally defined according to the potential of broad public debate for social utility, and that suitable limits may be determined in legal practice by institutional procedures and in the circumstances through which expressions or statements of individual claims have arisen and been made public. Hence one is often led to feel that in his function as citizen a Frenchman is never more satisfied than when circumstances provide occasions and settings for political confrontations. He is satisfied not only because his sense of form, clarity, and meaning is thereby given play, but because such confrontation cuts through all those complex matters of institutional hierarchy, function, and place that are so necessary to physical existence. Confrontation politics raises all men to that realm of abstract equality, and hence also of solidarity, where those who believe as we do are brothers, and all those who believe as the State does are the fallen.

One aspect of this notion of human rights is the paradoxical position in which it leaves the courts. Nominally, they should be agents of a state whose essential function is to give particular expression to the general moral sense. Practically, they offer a forum of ritual confrontation between citizen and power that serves the deepest needs of both. Frenchmen thus tend to be both cynical about the kind of justice offered in the courts and just as inclined to be litigious. And this paradox has its cultural basis in the importance attributed to rules and forms which, however wrong they may appear to those whom they oppress, at least result from human intention, and thereby rise above the level of historical accident and the processes of un-self-conscious social existence. As for the courts themselves, they have reflected these attitudes of cynicism and the desire for confrontation according to their own traditions and procedures, of which those associated respectively with each of the dual jurisdictions are perhaps the most striking.

Since we have seen something of the ways in which the administrative courts define the *régime préventif*, of setting limits on the official use of prior restraint, and of the pains taken to distinguish between the tasks of the two sets of courts, it is now time to turn to the work of the regular courts in order to determine how they define the circumstances according to which statutory law takes on that weight of moral meaning which renders it legally obligatory to the private author and speaker.

CHAPTER FOUR

The Conventionality of
Legal Morals

Nothing in the law springs entirely from a sense of convenience. There are always certain ideas existing antecedently on which the sense of convenience works, and of which it can do no more than form some new combination; and to find these ideas . . . is exactly the problem.

Henry Maine, *Ancient Law*

The immediate application of a rule of law depends on circumstances. We have already seen how circumstances in the form of "clear and present dangers" guide French administrative law in its attempts to define the limits of prior restraint. In this chapter, I want to show the really different way in which the criminal and civil courts, with their concern for malice and negligence, take note of circumstances. For it is clear that "circumstances" are not only facts, but facts taken in a perspective which gives them certain legal meanings. And since with the French civil and criminal courts we shall discover that notions of clear and present dangers are not part of their modes of reasoning, we shall conclude that their processes are inherently "ideological."

Unlike the administrative judges, the judges of France's regular courts decide by attributing personal responsibility to author or agent of the speech act. It is therefore a moral perspective alone that can provide the bench with a means for identifying such knowledge of right or wrong by which the existence and degree of the author's liability may be assessed. As we shall see in the cases to follow, discovery of intent is a key to application of such a moral perspective.

How does this key work, and what is its nature? Specific examples will help answer these questions. But it must be noted that the legal nature of the key is formal and abstract; no court is interested in what the agent was really thinking when he expressed such and such an opinion. What it needs to know is how the opinion can be made to compare with a highly conventional view of moral life, to which the judges themselves give expression by the way in which they see the circumstances in each case.

My first case shows the abstractness of legal intent well. In June, 1961, in the town of Cambrai, the manager of a local movie theatre was charged with the misdemeanor of an offense against decency, under Article 38, section 9 of the Criminal Code. According to the judge of the police court in which the case was heard, the manager, Monsieur de Quental

> . . . did affix to the walls of this town, at the time of the showing of the film *La bride sur le cou* (roughly translatable as "Free Rein") a number of posters, reproduced by photo-offset process, of the actress Brigitte Bardot, a film starlet, standing in the pose of Ingres's painting "La Source" and entirely unclothed except for a small G-string, hands crossed over breast, like a surprised nymph. . . .[1]

Were these posters "contrary to decency" in terms of the law? The charge had been brought against M. de Quental on complaint of the president of the Family Association of Cambrai, who had found the pose and the relative state of undress of the model improper in light of his duties to the young.

As to the law, the court had to respond to three questions raised by counsel for the defense. First, did not the fact that the poster had received approval from the Ministry of Commerce and Industry as suitable for advertising wholly excuse de Quental from any possible wrongdoing? Second, did not the absence of malicious intent on the defendant's part flaw the indictment fatally? And third, could it really be said that the poster was indecent in this day and age?

The judge disposed of the first two questions quickly. Administrative permission does not constitute the "permission of the law." Hence, approval of the poster by the appropriate administrative agency could not excuse wrongdoing. And as to the question of intent, the Ministry of Justice had already settled that matter by a circular of January 23, 1956 concerning posters contrary to decency:

> The infraction is not a matter of moral intention but of municipal administration, and the protection and good order of public thoroughfares.

Moreover, according to the judge,

> offenses against morals are punishable whatever the motives of their author, those of the accused in this case being evidence not of a desire to attack decency but to assure profitable receipts at the box office by means of provocative publicity.

As a consequence, the only hope for a verdict of innocence had to lie with de Quental's third plea, to the effect that the poster was not in fact indecent. To deal with the issue on its merits, the judge began by noting that

> decency is essentially a relative concept which in a given period is valued according to the environment of that period. . . Thus, although it is true that during the summer today's swimming pools and beaches offer the spectacle of young women in costumes not perceptibly more ample than that of the actress on the poster in question, and without these young women being embarrassed or self-conscious, it is nonetheless evident that their appearance would be judged indecent if by chance they were seen in the same clothing in the public garden or on the streets of Cambrai or elsewhere in the majority of French towns, and that they would thenceforth be promptly conducted via patrol car to the nearest police station. . . . Now the incriminated pos-

ters were placarded precisely along such streets and other places where they were clearly seen by passers-by. Hence the picture must be judged as if it were a living model in the same place.

Time and place may thus be seen as the hinge on which decision was to turn. But we are not now dealing with the same considerations of time and place as those of the administrative courts, despite the reference to the "good order" of the public thoroughfare. Here, instead, time and space define a conventional moral context, to which the social sensibilities of de Quental should have been attuned. This context was further spelled out by the court as follows:

> [Defense] cannot depend on reference to nude statues in public squares and gardens, because their nudity is an integral part of the nature and design of these public places. . . . They are works of art which go beyond carnal reality and which spiritualize the human body, and thus do not really involve considerations of decency or indecency. To take a typical example, the sculptor Bartholomé was able, without anyone's being shocked, to arrange nude figures of both sexes and all ages on the walls to the monument to the dead in the Père-Lachaise Cemetery. Conversely, whatever the technical quality of the poster in question, it can hardly be considered a work of art, and the body of the actress is certainly not given a "spiritual" interpretation.
>
> Indeed, the indecency of her appearance is aggravated even more by the lewd pose emphasizing the areas of erotic fixation, by the impudence of her look, and one must add, by the sexually-charged charm associated with the model herself. Above all, the picture cannot be separated from the text of the poster and from its physical context, since the position of the subject's arms, combined with the injunction "Stick 'em up!" inscribed in the dialogue "balloon" of some shadowy partner, suggests another image the erotic value of which makes further comment unnecessary.
>
> The indecency required to justify the prosecution is there-

fore sufficiently established in this case, despite the apparent inaction of public prosecutors and the indifference of public opinion in other towns where the same poster was displayed. Hence, the third argument is no more firmly grounded than the previous two. . . .

However, since this is a first offense, and the granting of the administrative permit, by which [the defendant] could have believed himself properly authorized to use the publicity material sent him by the film distributors, constitutes an extenuating circumstance . . . he will be given primarily a warning, and a moderate application of the penalty:

By these arguments—pronounce and judge de Quental guilty and convicted of the act charged, and condemn him to a fine of [$40] and expenses.

We see here that appreciation of the circumstances leading to decision in this case arises from a particular method for determining the demands of social convention. Had de Quental thought of the nude figures in the Père-Lachaise Cemetery? Did he even know such sculpture existed? When putting up the posters, had he imagined young ladies similarly dressed and present in the flesh, so to speak, in order to wonder whether they would have been "embarrassed and self-conscious" under such circumstances? Surely not! Yet his failure to make these or other appropriate comparisons in his imagination did not excuse his flouting Cambrai's assumed conventions of decency.[2]

The importance of a conventional moral view in such a case as de Quental's only points to the essential function of a kind of public opinion. As to what this kind can be in French criminal courts, let me give another illustration, also involving an advertising poster. Instead of Brigitte Bardot, more or less nude dancing girls were pictured in this one. The judges reacted as follows:

Whereas the variability of the notion of *bonnes moeurs* in time and place prevents us from using . . . the mentality of the last century as the source of our standards . . . it is nevertheless incumbent upon the courts to slow down the evolution of customs they deem contrary to the highest [conceptions of] morality, the rules of which have been perpetuated through long centuries, inscribed in the positive law, and reasserted again in our present statutes, for the purpose of checking certain debauched and corrupt habits, even where these are not necessarily shocking any longer to the majority of our contemporaries. . . . [On the other hand,] even for those to whom the instant poster may appear to go beyond the limits of permissible taste, it is not possible to affirm that the draftsman and printer . . . who produced the work, knowing that it would be put in public view, could have imagined that it was contrary to *bonnes moeurs.* All charges are therefore dismissed.[3]

Here we see a court pressing jobbers—draftsmen and printers—into service as representative of a certain moral opinion. If the bench had shared the workingmen's consciousness, would it have thought of the poster as shocking or scandalous? Would men of the workaday world, like draftsmen and printers, have risked their livelihoods for the sake of casually producing an indecent advertisement?

Now if conventions about community standards must dominate the legal definition of such concepts as obscenity and decency, how different is the situation where libel and slander are involved? Ever since 1887, when a court in Bourges decided that the epithet "Adulterer!" applied to a husband was an insult (*injure*) and therefore punishable without reference to specific facts, while applied to a wife was a libel that could be punished only when used in relation to an assertion of specific fact, it has been realized in France that much law depends on the mores of time and place even in realms beyond those of obscenity.[4] To illustrate how far beyond, let me turn now to the famous Frenay affair, which dates from 1945, when the spirit of the Liberation from Nazi occupation was at its most active.

In this case the charge of defamation was brought by the public prosecutor against Mme. Barron, a journalist, and M. Cachin, publisher of the Communist newspaper *l'Humanité* under Article 31 of the Press Law on behalf of Henry Frenay, then

Minister for War Prisoners and Displaced Persons. According to the indictment, Mme. Barron had wilfully and maliciously defamed Frenay concerning the conduct of his official duties.

These duties included finding and returning French deportees and POW's from Germany. According to *l'Humanité*, however, Frenay had failed to carry out these duties, not because of incompetence, but because of his political opinions. Mme. Barron specifically accused the plaintiff of having had nefarious contacts with Vichy officials, delayed repatriation for certain groups found in German concentration camps, rounded up 1300 exiles from the Spanish Civil War who had been active in the French Resistance to facilitate their enforced deportation to Spain, and delayed French acceptance of 857 Jewish orphans found in Buechenwald because of his anti-Semitism.

The key question decided by the court was not whether Frenay had been harmed by the articles. He clearly throught he had been, and the public prosecutor obviously agreed. The question was rather whether there had been enough truth in *l'Humanité's* assertions to make them valid political comment and thus discharge the defendants on the basis of their lack of malicious intent. Again, considerations of time and place were found critical. But again, these were not the same kind of time and place considerations as those dealt with by the administrative courts in their definition of police powers. The essential truth of the newspaper columns was rather found in the *moral* atmosphere of the time, which the court therefore went to considerable length to describe. The kind of truth the judges were concerned with in this case was therefore not of a physical but of an intellectual and moral order. It was by reference to this framework that the court reached the conclusion that the factual inaccuracies, including specifically the false attribution of political motive to Frenay, were legally excusable. In light of the moral context of the time, characterized by the bench as lacking those norms of civility ordinarily engendered by republican institutions, the intent of author and publisher had to be presumed innocent:

> Before examining the public acts which are the subject of these particular columns, it is appropriate to consider the

general atmosphere in which the criticism was offered, not only because of the circumstances surrounding their publication but also for the meaning of the law. . . . For this is a political law, which, in one observer's views, must be considered as "a beginning of the process of making amends to the human spirit, which the powers of government have ever tried to keep from communicating with mankind."

First, the Law of July 29, 1881, coming shortly after the victory of *le seize mai*, was promulgated during one of the most brilliant periods of the Third Republic, when the republican leaders, though odiously insulted and violently slandered by their monarchist, legitimist, orleanist, and bonapartist adversaries, nevertheless assured them impunity by refusing to call for repressive means: "They look for every way of dishonoring us," said Allain-Targé," . . . and we have not undertaken any action against them whatever; we haven't even used our pens to defend ourselves. Nor are we any the worse for it." Thus, although it did not create a regime of unlimited liberty inherent in republican ideology, which would be a liberty based on an absolute right of freedom and the complete impotence of repression, the Law of July 29, 1881, did nevertheless make great progress toward abrogating *délits d'opinion*, and it has therefore long been the best guarantee of the continuation of the democratic regime. Because of serious excesses of the period, however, penal provisions inherited from previous legislation were added. But they have rarely been applied to ministerial acts.

Second, between 1940 and the Liberation, though the de facto government . . . suppressed the press opposing Germany and controlled the rest to the point of making it entirely subservient, it was not able to silence the country's aspirations for freedom. During this unhappy period, when the slightest patriotic gesture was called an attack on the security of the State, the regime established and protected by Germany had no use for the Law of July 29, 1881, while the clandestine press flowered—inspired, edited, printed, and distributed by ardent patriots who were not frightened by threats of death. . . . Only this press permitted the People to express their joys and angers in the very face of the invader and an unworthy government.

Third, although the Committee of National Liberation kept faith with French traditions by reestablishing, as early as May 6, 1944, one of the fundamental liberties of the Republic, freedom of the press, the behavior of the popular press could hardly change from one day to the next, the People having lost their ability to chose their epithets, their formulae, their reasoning. Furthermore, ministerial acts, not then being submitted to parliamentary control, could not enjoy in the eyes of public opinion all the moral authority ordinarily adhering to decisions made democratically through a system of ministerial responsibility to representtatives elected by the Nation. And, when, for reasons of patriotism or gratitude for the work undertaken by our leaders, there was a tendency among some Frenchmen, in the face of the exigencies of the time, to restrain themselves from speaking out about their political ideals, we need not be surprised that certain newspapers tried to influence governmental decisions in matters where principles dear to their hearts appeared to be in question, such as the humanitarian mission of France, the public school, the protection of the weak, the care of children, old people, etc. . . . It is in light of these historical circumstances that we must judge the political behavior of the press, in this matter where the bench is sovereignly responsible for determing the facts, and when the line between legitimate criticism and illicit allegation is often hard to find, and is always more delicate where questions of a governmental nature are involved. . . .

At this point, the opinion examined the actual assertions of the newspaper columns in question against the facts as reported in the court's findings. In each case, the judges concluded that to have imputed any of the acts to the personal wishes of the plaintiff himself was inexact, but that *l'Humanité* was by no means entirely in error to report them, since officials in Frenay's department might appear to bear some responsibility for their occurrence. The court thus concluded:

While the indicted articles were perhaps a bit sharp (*vifs*) because of the polemics then common, and do no doubt present some inaccuracies of detail for which the minister could have used his right of public correction (*droit de rectification*—Article 12 of the Press Law), they contain neither defamation nor insult. All charges are therefore dismissed and the plaintiff is rebutted in his suit . . . all expenses being at his charge.[5]

If the most notable feature of the Frenay decision was the judges' very self-conscious attempt to characterize the spirit of the time, that time can hardly be said to be typical. I want now, therefore, to take a case that did not flow so directly from national events as did Frenay's, but that arose from a very ordinary kind of situation. Beginning in November, 1955, the weekly newspaper *La Presse* began a series of articles under the title: "French Consumers Protest: Give Us Our Daily Bread (and Not Our Daily Poison)".[6] The theme of these columns has long since been familiar. They made a broad attack on the increasingly industrial processes used in the manufacture of bread, with special reference to the chemicals used in yeasts and mildew preventives.

Yet for all their familiarity, these articles in particular gave umbrage to one baker, a M. Paques of Châlon-sur-Marne, and to four different associations representing bread producing —the National Confederation of Bakers, the Association of Wheat Producers, the Syndic of Makers of Yeast, and the National Association of French Millers. All brought suit under both the criminal provisions of the Press Law and Article 1382 of the Civil Code against *La Presse* and its editor and publisher, Monsieur d'Almeida.

In rendering judgment, the *Tibunal civil de la Seine* first dismissed all criminal charges under the Press Law, finding that the author of the columns in question could hardly have meant the expression "to poison oneself at the bakery" in a literal sense, any more than his use of the term to "traffic" in grains meant that dealers of the raw materials of bread were doing anything else than "negotiating" in them. Nor did the court find that *La Presse* had accused any part of the industry of not adhering to the "extremely close legal and administrative regulations" concerning the handling of bread's component elements. In the court's view, therefore, the question of the case was whether the various plaintiffs had suffered a material and/or moral injury for which the publisher and his publishing house could be held *civilly* liable.[7]

In order to determine the defendants' negligence, the judges turned, not surprisingly, to a consideration of circumstances. On the one hand, these were characterized by the banality of M. d'Almeida's theme:

> It is doubtless appropriate to note that the overall tenor of the essays in question is to take up the hackneyed challenge to machines and progress in general, while deploring the disappearance of the artisan's old techniques. And though it is hardly forbidden to be nostalgic about wheat raised in the good old earth by means of organic fertilizers, flour ground in a windmill, yeast prepared by the baker himself, bread kneaded by hand and baked in an oven heated by wood, surely the time when Jean Macé wrote his *Histoire d'une bouchée de pain* has largely passed. The necessity of of feeding ever greater masses of people, while at the same time lessening mankind's workload, necessarily requires the use of techniques which can hardly avoid having some unfortunate consequences on the quality of certain products.

So negligence could not be found in nostalgia per se. One had to ask whether the kind of charge made against the technology of bread production had any legitimacy at all. As the court put it:

> So far as bread, which is a basic element in feeding the nation, is concerned, it is well known that many books and articles written by doctors, hygienists, and dietitians have rightly or wrongly taken up the same theme, some even going so far as to maintain that the decline in the quality of bread is responsible for the development of certain illnesses, including especially cancer. Even when based on

empirical observations, however, these theories have never taken on such a broad and affirmative character as to justify some of the phrases used by *La Presse* . . . , such as in the headline itself first . . . and then in the text: "In our time, bread has become a dreadful poison, the cancer-causing agent par excellence"; "The consumer can thus with full assurance poison himself at his baker's"; "It goes without saying that the baker himself is in no way responsible for the systematic poisoning of the consumer . . . ;" "Without doubt, those who traffic in wheat and flour are afraid that the consumer will be able to tell the difference only too easily, and thus abandon for good the infamous paper paste he is offered today under the name of bread."

While the defendant cannot be reproached for having joined this campaign and reflecting such concerns, and even for making certain accusations, it is nevertheless true that none of the documents produced by the defense—even where they constitute a note of alarm, like the declaration of Professor Thuhaut of the Paris School of Pharmacy at the International Congress on cancer, which pointed to, among many other possible causes of cancer (industrial smoke, chemical insecticides, feed used in fattening cattle and poultry, use of plastic containers for foodstuffs) the discovery of certain deposits of carcinerogenous soot on bread baked in some types of direct heat ovens—permits the making of such a categorical assertion concerning bread as that it is the "cancer causing agent par excellence."

"Tendentious and hazardous" these assertions may have been, were they alone enough to engage d'Almeida's liability? Perhaps not, because later in its opinion the court seems to have found the critical factor to lie in an indication of a particular state of mind on the part of the articles' author. This indication lay in a reference to what he called the "disastrous affair of Pont-Saint-Esprit." From this phrase, the judges seem to have inferred the author's intention to misrepresent facts thus showing his wilfull negligence with respect to journalism's unwritten code of ethics.

The Pont-Saint-Esprit affair had involved the bread poisoning of a substantial number of people in that village in 1952.[8] Official inquiries had concluded that although the cause of the poisoning could not be conclusively determined, no evidence of human malice or negligence could be found. For this reason, d'Almeida's judges went on:

> while *La Presse* . . . has the right to recall such serious accidents and to remind public authorities and professional organizations of the need for precautions in the handling and transport of flour so that any risk of contact with toxic materials may be avoided, its summary reference to the "disastrous affair of Pont-Saint-Esprit" without any mention of the results of the inquiry showing that conditions of storing and preserving wheat had nothing to do with the poisoning in that affair, surely constitutes a remark quite without foundation and particularly biased in its attempt to make up the reader's mind by the repeated use of the words "poison" and related terms. . . .
>
> Therefore, however necessary and salutary newspaper campaigns alerting the public to dangers it ought to know about may be, it is nevertheless incumbent upon the journalist who undertakes such a campaign not to abandon a constant care for exactitude and objectivity. And while it may on occasion be excusable, when borne along by the pen, to use a slightly stronger or less nuanced expression than the state of his information permits, he may not, without making himself guilty of imprudence and thoughtlessness, and without engaging his civil liability, put forth as certain such grave assertions as the one which characterizes modern bread as a "dreadful poison" and the "cancer-causing agent par excellence."

The court thus found in favor of the plaintiffs on the basis of "at least a moral prejudice, and perhaps ultimately a material one, for which reparation is owed." But we may ask whether the judges' mode of argument here does not reflect a greater concern for reassuring the public with respect to the alertness of the public authorities than for protecting the interests of the plaintiffs. The court's sentence itself can be interpreted, in any case, as responding to both concerns. It ordered *La Presse* to publish in its own pages the complete text of the judicial decision against it, and it allowed the plaintiffs to publish, at the defendent's expense, and if "need be by abstract, this judgment in ten newspapers in France . . . the cost of no one of these notices to exceed ($85)."

To show other ways in which French courts have sought to discover guilty intent, I want now to turn to cases of slander of public institutions. The historical weight of French law here is great. Not only is there a tradition of treating defamation involving private persons as a matter of criminal, and thus public, concern, there is also a traditon of regarding public institutions in terms of their symbolic value, and verbal attacks upon them as inherently subversive. This burden to free speech no doubt had its origin in the once close association in French history between church and state. When the Revolution came to propagate a new republican dogma, it strengthened the forms of the earlier perspective even as it destroyed their particular historical manifestations.

The Press Law continued something of the old view in its articles 26, 29, 30, and 31, with the specific limitation provided for in Article 35, that proof in court of defamatory facts relating to all public functions, and to those private ones which solicited funds and credit from the publice, should constitute grounds for the immediate dismissal of all charges. Article 26, however, speaks only of *offense* to the President of the Republic, *not* of defamation, so that prosecutions under this head may be undertaken without reference to the notion of fact, as we shall see. And Article 29 specifically defines insult (*injure*)—"an outrageous expression, term of disdain or invective containing no imputation of fact"—in such a way that a defense based on proof is out of the question, thus rendering prosecutions for insult against public agents and institutions potentially quite easy. The Frenay case above suggests that courts have on occasion been reluctant to let these repressive measures get out of hand, the presumption of innocence lying very much with the defendant when the plaintiff is an ordinary public official. But Article 226 of the Penal Code, under which defendant Schroedt in the following case was prosecuted, makes no allowance for such a presumption because it punishes "whosoever, by public acts, words, or writing, seeks to throw discredit on any judicial act or decision in conditions of such a nature as to bring harm to the authority or independence of justice . . .

Schroedt was publisher of a union newspaper called *Voix Ouvrière*, and in one of his editorials he attacked a decision of Montbéliard's *Conseil des prud'hommes*. Montbéliard is the seat of Peugeot's major factory and *Conseils des prud'hommes* are courts of arbitration in labor-manager relations. In this affair, the *Conseil des prud'hommes* of Montbéliard had been called on to settle a dispute arising from Peugeot's firing of four shop stewards for having illegally engaged, so management said, in union activities on the plant floor. Since labor and management have an equal number of representatives in the *Conseils*, it had been necessary to call in one more judge (*juge départiteur*) to decide the dispute. This man cast his vote with management, thus legalizing the firing of the shop stewards. In an editoral in *Voix Ouvrière* Schroedt responded this way:

> Management has been authorized to fire four shop stewards. This is a parody of justice, by a Peugeot court. . . . By their judgments they strike down those who have the courage to oppose the bosses of the system. . . . We ought to react against such a decision. . . . This kind of justice is nothing but big business justice.[10]

In bringing suit under Article 226 in the *tribunal correctionnel* at Montbéliard, the public prosecutor rushed to the defense of the system where he believed it to be most threatened—in the minds of the public:

> To assert that justice is in the hands of management, to speak of a "Peugeot court," to maintain that now, "as in the age of tyrants and kings, they strike down those who have the courage to stand up against the guys on top," this is to

libel; and to libel in such a way as to cause harm to the authority and independence of our system of justice. Because what confidence in justice will anyone have if he believes, on the strength of the assertions in *Voix Ouvrière*, that the judges take their orders from big business . . . ?

Certainly if it were left up to ourselves, we would treat the libel published by *Voix Ouvrière* with disdain. But would not failure to react run the risk of seeing not simply false but really dangerous ideas get planted in the minds of its readers? Could we let the thesis that judicial decisions are supremely wicked and dictated to the courts by the great industrial corporations gain credit with the public, which is always inclined to believe what is printed and not formally denied? We have thought not.

In finding Schroedt guilty as charged, the *tribunal correctionnel* gave rather different reasons. Its decision turned not only on what it called the "manifestly malicious and insulting character" of Schroedt's editorial, but also on its finding that his desire to "descredit the decision of the *Conseil des prud'hommes* in the minds of the workers" was meant to "incite them to take action to cause it to fail. . . ." The bench specifically rejected Schroedt's principal argument, which had aimed at broadening the scope of circumstances in such a way as to render the expression of his criticism merely conventional:

It is in vain that defendant maintains that he did not write with malicious intent because the views he expressed were in keeping with Marxist theory. For in fact he did not deliver a doctrinal attack on "bourgeois" justice in its essential character, but rather a perfidious and slanderous attack on a particular court decision. Wherever his political loyalties may lie, in any case, the defendant had the duty to observe a certain measure in the expression of his opinions, and to limit the terms of meaning of the materials he published. Finally, the admitted fact that he had not even read the decision of the *Conseil des prud'hommes* before writing his article shows his bad faith, and his deliberate intent to go beyond the limits of objective criticism. Schroedt is therefore guilty of the charge against him, but is accorded, by reason of his previous good behavior, the benefit of extenuating circumstances. . . . He is sentenced to pay a fine of [$100].

Bigger fish than Schroedt are sometimes engaged in attacks on public institutions, although they are probably less likely to find themselves punished for it. The following case speaks for an exception. It constitutes the other half of the story of administrative seizure, recounted in Chapter III, of Fabre-Luce's book *Haute Cour*, and the *offense* contained therein to President de Gaulle. Article 26 of the Press Law recalls those attempts of the kings of the *ancien régime* to protect authority from all expression of disrespect. But its more recent antecedents are to be found in those laws passed during the nineteenth century, the dates of which reflect "restoration" of some king or emperor: 1815, 1848, 1853. The original draft of the Press Law bill contained a provision that would have protected not only the President of the Republic but the Republic itself and the two houses of Parliament from *offenses*. But with fine Radical temper, the Chamber refused to accept protection against insult for itself, the Senate, or the Republic. That left only the President of the Republic.

It then remained to be seen how the courts would interpret the term *offense*. At the turn of the century it was decided that in order to constitute *une offense*, the expression used would have to be either abusive or contemptuous. When a bystander shouted at President Loubet in 1902 as the Presidential carriage rolled by, "Resign! Down with Loubet!" the judges found him guilty. A more recent court reached the same decision when the same words were addressed to President de Gaulle. In the later case the fine amounted to about $100.

There has nevertheless been a considerable difference between the Fifth Republic's use of Article 26 and that of previous regimes. From 1881 to 1958 the law was invoked, so far as I can tell, nine times. Under de Gaulle's Presidency, the same provision was invoked more than 300 times. This enormous disparity does not mean that President de Gaulle was a great deal more sensitive to criticism than his predecessors. The change is due rather to the fact that since 1962 the office itself has been much more interesting target than it was when Clemenceau remarked that the two most useless organs in nature were the prostate gland and the President of the Republic, and advised his fellow electors on the occasion of a presidential ballot to "vote for the stupidest." In short, the change of status of the Presidency under the Fifth Republic turned what was seemed a minor provision into a major constitutional issue.

The first line of defense of those who have been charged with violation of Article 26 under the Vth Republic has been the argument that the law was obviously intended to apply only to a figurehead chief of State, not to a political officer, and certainly not to the most important political figure in the nation. In order to be true to the spirit of republicanism today, so this argument has gone, the courts should now recognize broad criticism of the President to be a matter of legitimate political discussion, and employ a far more restrictive definition of the term *offense* than may previously have been appropriate.

The courts have yet to accept this argument, however. The closest they have come to a concession on this point was expressed in a 1965 opinion:

> Though nothing may be opposed to the right of an author to criticize, even sharply, the policy of the President of the Republic, and to recommend another, this liberty may not degenerate into license to attack the very person of the Head of State himself, to insult him, to attempt to heap opprobrium upon him or to impute unworthy motives to him.[11]

Although this statement seems to decide the constitutional question, it does nothing to say what kinds of remarks may legally constitute an attack "on the very person of the Head of State," and for this reason I offer the decision of the trial of Fabre-Luce.

The circumstances of this case were determined by the plot of *Haute Cour* itself, for the substance of Fabre-Luce's criticism

117

of the General were hardly unusual. On the contrary, it was the common coin among critics of the regime. This left the question of its form and style. That Fabre-Luce is an historian of repute perhaps casts some light on the matter. For if, as an historian, he had laid out the same charges against de Gaulle as those actually contained in *Haute Cour*, if he had merely reported some of the well-known views on de Gaulle, held by well-known, nonfictional personages whom he had make fictional appearances in his imaginary story, all in the form of a straightforward nonfictional history, it seems unlikely that the court would have found means for condemning his book. The means grew out of the fact the Fabre-Luce had adopted as the framework of *Haute Cour* the particular fiction of a hypothetical treason trial in which President de Gaulle himself was the accused. This approach seemed to the court to demonstrate guilty intent precisely because of its imaginary character.

In this finding we may sense again a certain conventionality in the judges' perspective: "surely there are things which are simply not said," perhaps particularly if everyone has already heard about them. It was apparently this kind of limit that the court meant to hold Fabre-Luce and his publisher to, perhaps all the more that both were equally respected and respectable. Here are excerpts from the judges' decision:

> The [plot] supposes that by the procedures of Article 68 of the Constitution, the Head of State has been impeached by a vote of the two Houses of Parliament, but that at the opening of the trial the new Government has modified the composition of the High Court so that it consists thereafter, as was the case in the Third Republic, of the Senate alone. [The story] then proceeds in six chapters to reproduce an imaginary stenographic account of the six hearings of the affair, accompanied by a commentary from one of the witnesses at these hearings, who from time to time interrupts the stenographic account to give his own "impressions."
>
> By this means the reader learns that the General is under indictment on the following counts:

(1) Abandonment of the national territory, punishable under Article 86 of the Penal Code;

(2) Undertaking a plot to demoralize the Nation, punishable under Article 84 of the same code;

(3) Violation and betrayal of the duties of his office in such conditions as to constitute high treason, punishable under the terms of Article 166 of the Penal Code.

As the trial proceeds, the reader is confronted with depositions from various witnesses, both for the prosecution and the defense. Sometimes these witnesses are real people (former ministers, members of Parliament, members of the academies) to whom Fabre-Luce claims to have attributed remarks actually made by them, and in some cases fictional characters (an historian, a politician, a judge of the Council of State, the Prosecutor of the High Court, etc. . . .) who, the author writes, "have been given roles appropriate to their place in the trial, but who in no instance affirm any facts which are inexact."

The book also reproduces hypothetical briefs of prosecutor and defense, the author stating that in light of his respect for the Head of State he does not attribute to him the "kinds of declaration for which he is well known," but has him, after the manner of other notorious persons under indictment, such as Gamelin, Pétain, and Salan, maintain silence, refusing even to choose counsel, which has therefore been assigned him by the head of the bar.

The book ends at the moment when the Presiding Judge of the High Court is about to read the Court's judgment. The author refuses to reveal what it is, however, in order that "each reader may decide for himself what the verdict must be."

Fabre-Luce denies wishing to insult the President of the Republic in this work, which he describes as a literary one, and as a "novel as true to life as possible." He claims to have conducted himself in the manner of an historian, indicating in the postface his written sources. And in the preface he writes:

It is as an historian that I have put this dossier together. Every worthwhile argument had been set forth, and no conclusion prejudged. . . . Behind every line of this work there is a text, and many of them are confirmed by witnesses with whom I have personally talked.

But the very act of describing a fictional trial of the President of the Republic before a court that . . . can sit only in judgment of high treason constitutes of itself an insult to the Head of State. And this abusive supposition is further aggravated by supposing an indictment consisting of three counts, each of which is punishable under the Penal Code—one by civic degradation, and the other two by this and corporal punishment as well.

The book provides its author with an occasion, furthermore, to place in the mouths of fictional personnages abusive statements . . . and imputations or allegations of a kind to throw disdain on the person of the President, bring him into disesteem, and bear the greatest harm to his honor and reputation.

Thus, for example, the author makes a fictional former civil servant in Algeria say: "Fidelity rewarded by treason! That's all the European and Moslems who were loyal to France got out of his high policy." Nor does Fabre-Luce draw back from having this same personnage insinuate that General de Gaulle would have brought about the assassination of the rebel general Salan had not the latter, in an audience with the President, appeared disposed to persuade his comrades to lay down their arms, but who, "if we decide to give power to the National Liberation Front, will be nothing but a troublemaker."

The author also has this same personnage accuse the Head of State of having hoodwinked the Army, and of making it stand surety for his lies (p. 92).

Somewhat further on, the author has another witness, supposedly a *maître des requêtes* of the Council of State, claim that the President's authority is a "power of law that authorizes on the basis of a claimed legitimacy only in order to get around legality" (p. 131), and has him say in addition: "He makes us [members of the Council of State] do things in our public lives which we would never countenance in our private" (p. 136).

The author pushes lack of decency so far as to bring to the witness stand a psychiatrist who for more than eight pages sketches a particularly insulting portrait of General de Gaulle, whom he classifies psychologically as being "in the family of paranoiacs" (p. 181), depicting the General as a person imbued with himself, prompt to overestimate his capacities, imagining himself an infallible prophet, having nothing but disdain for his closest associates, and who, in the last years of office, is alleged to have arrived at a stage called "stereotyped," indicated by the frequent use of the same gestures, words, tics, and so on . . . and thus approaching a period of "final and irreversible disintegration of the personality" (p. 193). This same psychiatrist concludes his testimony with these words: "Charles de Gaulle is not positively morbid, but his is not normal either. He is abnormal 'on top' rather that 'down below' " (p. 195). The psychiatrist then stigmatizes "the corruption of the public spirit under the influence of this personality" (p. 197).

The summation of the prosecution before the High Court provides the author with further occasions to deliver himself of abusive attacks. . . .Thus the Public Prosecutor, speaking of the acts of General de Gaulle during the War and at the time of the Liberation, is made to say: "General de Gaulle, you intimidated the French with your bluffing, and you profited from this intimidation to make yourself Head of State (p. 203) . . . Naturally as fallible as other men, your pride only made you more so (p. 204). You had to monopolize power, even if the nation had to suffer grievously for it" (p. 206). The Prosecutor also accuses the President of having committed "Creon's crime" by forbidding adherence "to those laws which since Sophocles' time have been called unwritten" and which demand that "we not renege on our solemn promises, that we not change the meaning of words, that we not humiliate those

121

whom it has been our privilege to command, that we not tear men away from their homes or the dead away from the land where they are buried" only to cry out, "You did all these things!" (p. 223-24). Finally, the author also has the Public Prosecutor accuse General de Gaulle of having shaken the very foundations of public ethics (p. 216), demoralized the nation, and been the chief cause of the civic perversion of the young.

Whereas neither the fact that the Public Prosecutor finally abandons the first two counts of the indictment, to ask only for a "moral punishment" called "National Obloquy," which a special law, passed for the circumstances, would have allowed the High Court to substitute for civic degradation as the punishment for high treason, nor the facts that the author has taken care to juxtapose witnesses in favor of General de Gaulle with those against him and the summation for the defense with the prosecution's, can be considered as effacing the wilfully insulting character exhibited both by the book's theme and by the abusive and defamatory passages cited above—all the less since the latter aspects of the work are confirmed by occasional passages giving "impressions of the hearings" . . . in one of which General de Gaulle is ironically referred to as "the Lord's annointed on the throne of infamy," and in another as a "fat walrus they're trying to capture."

Under these circumstances it is right to declare Dame Julliard, publisher of this book, guilty of the delict of public insult to General de Gaulle, and Fabre-Luce, author of said book, accomplice in this infraction. . . . For these reasons . . . and applying Articles 23, 26 paragraph 1. 42 and 43 of the [Press Law], 56 and 60 of the Penal Code, this court sentences each to a fine of [$300]; and by application of Article 61 of the same law, orders the seizure and destruction of all copies of the book *Haute Cour* wherever they may be put on sale, distributed, or exposed to public view; and sentences Dame Julliard and Fabre-Luce conjointly to all expenses. . . .[12]

Since we are now considering "circumstances" in political affairs, let us turn to cases that have arisen under what have turned out to be the most obviously political sections of the Press Law —its Articles 23, 24, and 25. As I wrote in Chapter II, these articles were fruit of a feeling among the majority of the legislators in 1881 that the *droit commun* would not be altogether appropriate for repressing bad ideas. It was said at the time, you will remember, that applicable provisions of the codes would lead either to too much repression, or none at all, and that it was therefore necessary to distinguish in statute between speech acts and other kinds for which one could be held legally liable. But once incitement to riot or to an immediate crime was taken care of in Article 23, by making the speaker an accomplice of the crime, the legislators' did not provide a framework for a "clear and present danger" rule, nor even one like Judge Learned Hand's, according to which the courts would weigh the "gravity of evil against its improbability." On the contrary, the wording of the Press Law made it possible for jurisprudence to distinguish between maintaining order and maintaining law. And it is this potential which succeeding events have substantially developed.

The cases following under Articles 23, 24, and 25 therefore provide further illustration of the thesis that considerations of "clear and present dangers" have virtually no part to play in the modes of reasoning of the regular courts in free speech cases. This is not to say that such considerations do not perhaps exist somewhere in the backs of minds of the French judges; the Schroedt case suggests that they may be at times not very far below the surface. But because in France the law is not made from case to case, it is logical that a person should be held guilty only for his own maliciously intended acts, and not with a view to making his case profit the development of the law. For would it not be the greatest injustice to define a man's liability in terms either of the momentary dispositions of his fellowmen or other circumstances of time and place over which he has no control? There is, then, but one approach available to the determination of guilt or innocence in French courts where speech acts are concerned, and this approach is what is usually called in American legal circles the "bad tendency" test, after Blackstone:

To punish . . . any dangerous or offensive writing, which when published, shall upon fair and impartial trial be adjudged of *pernicious tendency*, is necessary for the preservation of peace and good order, of government and religion, the only solid foundations of civil liberty.[13]

Statutory warrant for a bad tendency approach is spelled out particularly in Articles 24 and 25 of the Press Law:

Article 24: Whosoever (by any means of public expression) does directly incite to theft or robbery, or to the felonies of murder, looting, arson , . . will, where such incitements has not been followed by its effect, be punished by from one to five years imprisonment and/or from ($60 to $60,000—approximate current scale) fine . . . Will be punished by the same penalties anyone who, [by any of the same means] makes an apology for [these same crimes] .
. . .
Article 25: Any incitement whatsoever [by any of these same means] which is addressed to soldiers of the army, navy, or air force for the purpose of dissuading them from their military duties and from the obedience they owe their superior officers in all that is commanded for the carrying out of military laws and regulations, will be punished (according to the same scale of fines and imprisonment).

Statutory warrant for a bad tendency approach is provided by these provisions because both explicitly exclude the judges from considering the real effects of a speech act. And application of the same penalties for "apologizing" for any of the enumerated felonies seems to go in the same sense. Indeed, the Press Law, as passed in 1881, effectively abrogated the law of September 8, 1835, that had made apology for a crime a punishable offense. It was only in response to the terrorist acts of Anarchists that the Law of December 12, 1893 reconstituted the delict of apology, at the same time limiting its application to the specific crimes of murder, pillage, theft, and bombing and omitting deliberately any reference to crimes against State security.

Yet the Law of December 12, 1893 responded specifically to a political threat, and its earliest uses consisted largely in prosecuting such statements as:

> We support the acts of Ravachol, Vaillant, Emile Henry, and everything else done in the name of anarchy. Far from repudiating what's going on in other countries, we thoroughly approve of them, especially the bombings in Barcelona. . . .

And

> Long live anarchy! Long live Ravachol![14]

If there had ever been doubt about this law's political import, however, it was dispelled by a change made through the Law of January 5, 1951. This act extended the list of crimes for which an apology itself would also be punishable to cover "crimes of war and of collaboration with the enemy," and was apparently added as moral compensation to the feelings of Resistance veterans, who were then agitated about a recent law of amnesty releasing collaborators from prison. If the Third Republic has its myth of *union sacrée*, The Fourth needed its myth of the Resistance, for General de Gaulle was not the only Frenchman to have "a certain idea of France." The only thing that Frenchmen seem able to agree on, however, is that whatever this "certain idea" may be, it is incarnated in specific institutions only at its, and their, peril. Thus, when the Radical Allain-Targé argued in 1881 that "there must always be a hopeless legal flimsiness in prosecutions concerning the press, because one has to hunt around among all possible courts and often dream up new ones in order to find judges whose minds are sufficiently supple to come to grips with human thought, and to uncover its real meaning beneath all the disguises it can wear. . . . "[15] he was stating only half the truth. The other half was, and is, that willingness to come to grips with thought, especially in its moral aspects, lies at the heart of French political life.

So far as the criminal courts are concerned, such willingness is nowhere better demonstrated than in cases where "apology" is at stake, as the four case to follow illustrate. The first of these, decided in 1907, concerned Victor Griffuehles, who was secretary-general of the *Confédération Générale de Travail* from 1898 to1914. No doubt the failure of his appeal to the Court of Cassation must be seen in light of the generally repressive view of French law and institutions with respect to working-class movements. As F. R. Ridley has put it, "The *loi Le Chapelier* (1796) forced the workers into opposition to the State; in a measure, indeed, it persuaded them to reject the State altogether . . . [an] attitude . . . reinforced by the memory of the great battles they had fought with the State in 1848 and 1871. . . . The labor movement built on the blood of its martyrs."[16] In Griffuehles's case, his legal troubles arose from a poster which the *C.G.T.* had placarded on the streets of Paris during a month when troops were being used to suppress street demonstrations in favor of workers' rights in general and in favor of those in the vineyards and bottling industry, which had been struck for months in the *Midi*, in particular.

The incident of which Griffuehles's posters made note soon became an element in the modern French revolutionary myth, celebrated in popular song and cabaret alike. All the more striking, then, that his judges found the message of his posters, which were placarded in the working class districts primarily, to have been directed at soldiers and thus to constitute an apology for the crime of military disobedience, an act whose delictuous nature could be decided without reference to probable, or even possible, effect. We can see in this early interpretation of Articles 24 and 25 a trend that in retrospect appears almost a leitmotif in the jurisprudence of the Third and Fourth Republics: a tendency to use the ethic of the military services, of their order and discipline, as a legal touchstone for identifying guilty intent. Griffuehles had appealed on a point of law: the term apology as used in Article 24, he argued, could not be applied to the message displayed on the *C. G. T.* posters. The judges of France's highest criminal court responded this way:

On June 23, 1907 certain posters were placarded in Paris and in the region of the Seine. They were printed so that

"General Confederation of Labor" appeared at the top, and just underneath "Government of Assassins." This poster contained in particular the following passages: "Police and soldiers have fired. Little difference does it make to us whether they fired under orders or not. Murder is still murder, and they fired. . . . Yet in the midst of these horrors one comforting fact came home to us. In a leap of conscience one regiment, the 17th of the Linne, held their rifle butts up in the air. . . . This gesture could only have been brief when it happened. But such as it was, it justified our antimilitarist propaganda. The peasants of the 17th have understood how right we are to proclaim that the bourgeoisie supports the army only in order to make war against the country itself." It is claimed in the appeal that the passages cited above cannot be considered as having constituted an apology for an act of disobedience on the part of soldiers, and that Article 24 of the [Press Law] . . . punishes only apology for the crimes and offenses of said article. But Article 25 . . . refers to any incitement addressed to the military for the purpose of dissuading them from their military duties. . . . It does not require that the incitement be direct. And since an apology for acts of disobedience committed by soldiers may present the character of an incitement to commit similar acts . . . such incitement, when addressed by any of the means enumerated in [the Press Law] to soldiers . . . falls under the provisions of Article 25 of said law.

Because the poster in question . . . was placarded on the walls of Paris there is sufficient reason to charge appellants with having . . . addressed an incitement to soldiers. . . . Their appeal is rejected.[17]

My next case arose in 1912, when defendants Keller and Bonafous, as publisher and editor of the newspaper le Libertaire, were charged with having made an apology for the violent crimes committed by the famous anarchist Bonnot, who had been killed in a shoot-out with police shortly before. The trial court had dismissed the charges on the ground that the eulogy for Bonnot which had appeared in *le Libertaire* did not constitute an apology for any specific crime, and thus did not fall under the provisions of the law which, being a criminal statute, had to be strictly interpreted. The public prosecutor had recourse to the Court of Cassation for a ruling on the matter of law, what did Article 24 mean by "apology"? The answer came down as follows:

A column entitled "The Death of a Man" in the newspaper *le Libertaire* contains the following passages:

It is not at the very moment when individuals are being fercociously hunted down by the most filthy of cops, at the very moment when the stinking [Prefect of Police] Guichard dreams of extending his mad activities to all lovers of liberty, it is not, I say, in the breathlessness of this struggle that we can stop to be precise about our own particular views. That Bonnot's logic was blindly, mercilessly implacable, so be it. It was nevertheless a scrupulous logic, exact, mathematical, that of an individualist, of a man who had the courage to go right to the very end of his views, to give a high affirmation of his revolt in the very face of a punishment he knew would be inevitable. . . . In the center, towering above the seething dwarfs who surrounded him, threatening and insulting him while they trembled to the very tips of toes, stood Bonnot. . . . living synthesis of all strength, all boldness, all scorn. . . . This is one thing Guichard and his ignominious band forgot to arrest in laying hold of Bonnot's corpse—it is the admirable lesson of will which emerges from the drama enacted at Choisey. Bonnot has shown us what one individual can do when he becomes conscious of his energy and aims it well—of that fruitful energy whose seeds are sleeping in the heart of all beings, only awaiting the occasion to affirm itself on the side of the noble idealism taught us by the fact that social iniquity perpetuates itself only because of the fears inspired by the minions of authority. In all the twists and turns of this ferocious battle Bonnot never lost his realism in pursuing his goal. The unequal struggle he undertook, the audacity of the wild beast which animated him, even when he recognized that he could be wrong, the certainty he had of dying in a horrible way—such a man, in approaching death, inspires not only pity but admiration for his courage, for his persistence in battle, for his tenacity in that uneven hand-to-hand struggle between himself and a whole society.

The passages above constitute an exaltation of Bonnot by reason of the crimes he committed. In these circumstances apology for the criminal is equivalent to the apology for the crimes committed by him, and thus falls under the purview of Article 24. . . .

For these reasons the lower court's dismissal of charges against Keller and Bonafous is quashed and annulled, and the parties and the cause are remanded to the Court of Appeals at Orleans. . . .[18]

My third illustration of the use of the concept of apology dates from the post-Liberation period, when the ministry in power seems to have made one Bardèche into a scapegoat for the broad amnesty that released many collaborators from prison in 1950. He had written a book in 1948 called *Nuremburg ou la terre promise*. But only in 1951 was he charged on that account with infraction of Article 24 of the Press Law by reason of the apologies his book allegedly contained for the war crimes of the Nazis. (The Law of January 5, 1951 had made apology for war crimes a part of the list of crimes of Article 24.) The trial court dismissed the charges against Bardèche on the ground that although his attacks on Jews, the conduct of Allied leaders during the war, the Nuremburg Trials, and the Resistance were "odious" and "of a nature to provoke indignation on the part of the public conscience," it could find nothing in the text specifically constituting an apology for the crime of murder. The prosecutor appealed to the Paris Court of Appeals, which reversed, and sentenced Bardèche to about $250 fine and one year in prison. Bardèche then appealed to the Court of Cassation, arguing that since his book nowhere contained passages excusing murder or other crimes, and explicitly condemned the crimes for which the Nuremburg defendants were brought to trial, the indictment must fail for lack of proof of malicious intent. Excerpts from the Court of Cassation's opinion follow:

Examination of the book shows . . . quite independently of its exaltation of the Nazi regime and . . . its defamatory references to the judges and prosecution of the Nuremburg tribunal, that the text, whose author declares himself to be addressing particularly the youth of Germany, does tend to justify generally the crimes committed by . . . German military and civil officials during the last World War, crimes which consisted largely of murder and assassination and which were recognized and punished as such either by the aforementioned international tribunal or by various courts of the Allied nations, and notably by French military tribunals.

In order to accomplish this justification, the author sets himself the task of showing in a general way that these crimes were either provoked by the attitude of the victims themselves or by that of their compatriots, so that the crimes were therefore only . . . legitimate means of defense. As a result, those who joined the Resistance and the Maquis, and other French patriots who took part in the fight against the enemy, were "provocateurs," guilty of having taken a frightful responsibility with respect to the civilian population from which, by their actions, they "withdrew all protection." On the same grounds, those who were deported, and who, according to the author, have since "more or less unconsciously turned their captivity into a useful thing" by substituting "for what they saw what it has become necessary to say," are similarly responsible for the sufferings they had to endure, because "they accepted or appeared to accept defense of the Jewish cause." Furthermore, the Jews themselves were largely responsible for their own massacre . . . because it was they who wanted the war: "they divided us, they demanded the blood of our best; they rejoiced at our deaths. By this war that *they* wanted, they have given us the right to say that it was their war." Consequently, their extermination was legitimate, because they thereby paid for the war that they themselves had brought about. . . . So "by right we don't have to count their deaths along with ours."

This book further attempts to justify these same war crimes by making it appear that they were only the legitimate response of the Nazi Reich to the so-called criminal

acts the Allies committed with respect to Germany. Bardèche declares, notably: "I will believe in the legal existence of
war crimes when I see General Eisenhower and Marshall
Rossokovksy take their place in the prisoner's box at
Nuremburg, and beside them some of the lesser figures, like
our General de Gaulle, who was responsible far more directly that Keitel or Jodl for a goodly number of atrocities." Or again: "As for me, the American Negro who
calmly pulls the bomb release over the houses of a German
city seems far more inhuman, still more monstrous, than
the prison guard who, in our imagery, accompanies the
Treblinsk victims to the fatal showers. And I confess
that if it were up to me to class Himmler, who set up the
concentration camps, and the British air marshall who
decided, one day in January of 1944 to order saturation
bombing, I think I would not put Himmler in first rank."
. . . By making this connection between Hitlerian procedures of extermination and the Allies' acts of war against
military objectives—especially since the author fails to
mention that the Allies were not the first to use such means
of war—the book ultimately exalts enemy criminals,
Bardèche himself specifically proclaiming: "I must say
that I have infinitely more respect for the moral courage
of SS General Olendorf, who frankly admitted that he had
killed 90,000 Jews and Ukranians on the orders of his
Fuehrer, than for the French general who caused as many
deaths, but who hasn't the guts to accept the responsibility."
Or again: "When we are reminded of this immense har-
vest of grandeur and sacrifice offered by young Germany
what shall we say—we, the accomplices of the judges, accomplices to the lies?"

Although it is true that in certain passages the author
says he disapproves of the crimes that he tries to justify in
the manner indicated above, this disapproval appears to
be little more than a device for giving greater force to his
main argument. So, for example, when he says that "we
like everyone else, condemn the systematic extermination
of the Jews," it is in order to add "that this extermination

was but one of the new methods of this war which we must judge in the same light as we judge the others including, especially, the bombing of German cities." And similarly, when he declares, "Of course, we condemn all methods of extermination, in all times, even in time of war," he continues by saying that the accusations against the German leaders have not been verified, and that in any case the Allies "had on their side systems of extermination just as extensive." In the same vein, when he admits that "it is sad to count our victims—77 at Ascq, 120 at Tulle, 800 at Oradour," it is to emphasize the minor importance of these killings in comparison with those suffered by the Slav populations. And when he expresses a certain indignation at the thought "of those unfortunate Ukranian women who had welcomed the German as liberators and were nevertheless stupidly massacred by them" it is in order to be able to add that his pain on this matter "coincides with the hypocritical feelings of Germany's accusers." And if he says "to the extent that the German army committed acts contrary to the laws of war" he condemns these acts and those who were responsible for them, his purpose is to claim that these were individual acts of which the Nazi leaders would have disapproved, and that in any case "these acts had been provoked by the attitude of the civilian population, the birth and development of Resistance groups, the attacks ordered by irresponsible organizations, Jewish propaganda and Communist action," so that "whatever the Germans responsibility in this matter may be, we must not forget that their adversaries were the first to put themselves in a position from which they had no right to claim the protection of international law." And if he recognizes that there are "incontrovertible war crimes," it is only the better to emphasize once again that responsibility for them is shared . . . even to arguing that "it is not only a band of brutes having lost all control of themselves who set fire to the church at Oradour, it is the man who used to speak on Radio London, and whose platform today is their tombstones."

In the light of these statements, the Court of Appeals did rightly find that by the methods of discussion analyzed above, and by the use of abusive comparisons, Bardèche did wilfully try to create confusion in the minds of his readers, and to lead them to a moral judgment favorable to Nazi criminals and their crimes. Even though he may not have been trying to glorify such crimes, therefore, the defendant's efforts to justify them do constitute an apology within the meaning of Article 24. . . . It makes no difference [furthermore], whether such crimes, having for the most part consisted of murder and assassination, be included under the general terminology of war crimes, for an apology made for them, even previous to the Law of January 5, 1951, is not the less punishable, since these crimes, not being justified by the laws and customs of war, fall under the provisions of Articles 295ff. of the Penal Code.

Finally, it is unnecessary to determine whether Bardèche did not intend, as he claims in his appeal, to provoke German youth, to whom he was especially addressing himself, or in a general manner his readers of other nationalities, to a renewal at some more or less distant time in the future of the atrocities whose legitimacy he upholds, because apology for a crime is an infraction distinct from incitement to crime. It is only necessary to verify, as the Court of Appeals did, that Bardèche wrote and published his book in knowledge of the definitions in French criminal law of apology for crimes described as murder or assassination. This determination establishes the wilful character of the infraction. . . .[19]

In our consideration of the way in which the moral framework of the community is asserted in law by the "bad tendency" approach to free speech, we have now seen how the idea of "apology" for a crime has served the purpose. I want to illustrate this point further, by citing a case where the imminence of the danger is again explicitly rejected in favor of treating the expression as inherently wrong in itself. The prosecution here was taken shortly after the Popular Front came to power, and the motives behind it are perfectly clear in relation to that event. The case arose from an article written by Charles Maurras for *l'Action française*, and both he and his publisher were brought to court on a charge of having violated Article 24 of the Press Law by their alleged recommendation of murder. The text of Maurras' column read as follows.

> We beg all good Frenchmen to take note of the 140 assassins of peace, assassins of France [these were 140 members of the French parliament who had signed a manifesto protesting Mussolini's attack on Ethiopia], to cut out the list . . . and if necessary to learn it by heart, in order to strike hard and firmly the day when these criminal mistakes lead to a massacre. . . . They no doubt hoped to get some advantage from signing. Let them also get the disadvantage. It will come to them the day the calls to mobilization fall like hail. And on that day it will be right that these men should expiate their crime. . . . The heart of the real country must, when it is bled by the legal country, know with certainty just who should suffer expiation. . . . Let us repeat to them that it is with their heads—with their heads, may they well understand—that the wretches must answer to us for peace. If peace lasts, they can keep the cervical apparatus which is so little use to them on their shoulders. But if peace succumbs, they too will succumb, one by one.

Defense counsel argued here that the text in question made Maurras' call for revenge against the 140 parliamentarians conditional to the coming of war, an eventually their clients no more wished for than did any of their countrymen. But this argument was explicitly rejected by the trial court, the Paris Court of Appeals, and the Court of Cassation, the last in particular saying,

> The judgment under appeal declared these passages to contain a direct instigation to the crime of murder, guilty

intent arising from the very terms used, and surabundantly established by the previous writings of Maurras. . . .The element of intent in this case resides in the fact of having wished to create the state of mind necessary to bring about the commission of the crime, regardless of the final goal or motive envisaged, and even though, in the author's mind, the instigation need not have been followed by immediate execution but be subordinate to a future hypothetical event or circumstance. . . . Defendants' appeal is thereby rejected.[20]

In light of the previous cases it is clear how effective a "bad tendency" approach can be in incriminating speech acts. So it is now time to ask what factors of a case may cause a prosecution to fail. The mode of reasoning of the Frenay affair having sprung from the rather unusual circumstances surrounding the dispute, I want here to offer a more "normal" example leading to the failure of a prosecution—normal in the sense that it specifically uses a general principle of French criminal procedure, the strict interpretation of criminal statutes. The case is that of Pierre Emmanuelli, once managing editor of a weekly called *La Provence nouvelle*. On May 15, 1949, his newspaper published an article whose theme has since become terribly familiar to Americans. The title of the column was "Demand an End to the Indochina War," and those passages selected by the State prosecutor as delictuous in terms of Article 76 (now Article 84), Sec. 3 of the Criminal Code and Articles 23, 24, and 25 of the Press Law, read as follows:

Frenchmen, die. Taxpayers, pay. That, in a few words, sums up the policy of the socialo-RPF Government. No honest Frenchman can doubt it. Officially, the Government is asking for 100 billion francs, but that is a minimum. And *France Industrielle* understands it well by announcing that the deficit for 1949 is already 150 to 200 billion. And we are barely in May! Who will pay the bill? The little shopkeepers, the peasants, the small businessmen, men and women of the independent professions, and, of course, the workers, who will be added to the ranks of the unemployed, because these billions will serve not to construct but to destroy. To destroy our youth in a dirty colonialist war. War against a people who has as much right to claim its independence as did the French when they fought against the Nazis. This war proves once again the subordination of French governments to American imperialism. This fact is recognized by the foreign affairs correspondent of *France-Soir*, Pertinax, who writes that General Revers will make a second trip to the United States "in hopes that the defense of Southeast Asia will be organized by the states with interests there. . . ." No! Not one more man! Not one more cent! Today this is the cry of all democrats, all Frenchmen who, joined together, must and can act immediately to force an end to this dirty, dirty war. . . .

The State prosecutor argued that this column constituted "knowing participation in an undertaking to demoralize the army and the nation in order to weaken national security," as proscribed by the Criminal Code, by one of the means enumerated in the Press Law. Having lost his case in the trial court, the prosecutor appealed. This is how the Court of Appeals of Aix-en-Provence responded:

First, Article 25 of the Press Law . . . requires that the instigation be directed to the military services by one of the means listed in Article 23. But the newspaper column in question is not directed to the military services. It is, rather, directed exclusively to the civilian population. Article 25 is therefore inapplicable. . . .

Second, the indictment charges . . . that instigation to crimes and misdemeanors against the external security of the State . . . has been undertaken, though not followed by any effect, and that consequently Article 76 of the Criminal Code is specifically applicable. . . . But this is . . . not so for the newspaper column on which the indictment rests, because by itself this column does not have the character of an undertaking to demoralize the army or the nation. It neither indicates to the reader, nor advises him of, the use of any means or method, limiting itself to a declaration that the French together "must and can act to force an end to this dirty, dirty war." Nor does the passage recommend the joining of or participation in any organization whatever having a technical activity or purpose that could be assimilated to "an undertaking" *(une entreprise)* as an application of the law would require. However open to criticism the act of the defendant may be in other terms, in matters of criminal law it is proper to give restrictive interpretations. Thus for lack of at least one of the elements necessary to the infraction as set forth in the indictment, it is according to law, and the statutes currently in force, that all charges against Pierre Emmanuelli were dismissed by the trial court, a judgment hereby confirmed.

So neither the remoteness nor imminence of any possible harm arising from the publication was at issue. The court looked only to the precise wording of the statutes, and found insufficient correspondence with Emmanuelli's message to establish guilt. His act simply was not one that the law forbid, "however open to criticism" it may have been. The fact that Emmanuelli's protest involved no practical recommendations for organizing opposition to the war may perhaps be taken as having some symbolic importance, because he must have known as well as the State prosecutor that their fellow-countrymen would never consciously unite in even the most remote circumstances concerning even the most hypothetical issue. In any case, the appeals court's refusal to find anything criminal in the newspaper passage by the means it did does strengthen one's impression that the *délit d' opinion*, so much disliked by the legislators of 1881, has in some measure been reconstituted, to the satisfaction not only of those in power and authority but perhaps even to that of the private citizen, who cannot fail to find some pleasure in the trouble the State may go to try to repress public expression of his ideas.

If this is so, as I should argue these cases show, then one must incline to the view that successive generations of Frenchmen have, even unto our own age, more or less chosen to distinguish between an idea of law as potential for perfect justice and an idea of order as claim of immediate utility. Of course this choice must in large part be a matter of institutional habit, for how many chances to begin again does history ever offer any nation? And yet France supposes herself to have taken more opportunities to begin again than most nations with democratic expectations. Few others, at any rate, have come to a point where they can regard their written constitutions as "periodical literature," as the long venerable joke has it. So if contemporary law men maintain and even elaborate the basic duality of the legal system, their activity may well reflect a cultural perspective concerning both the nature of rules and the meaning of liberty.

That this perspective involves a profound tension between law and order has been made evident. For the norms of the regular courts arise from a moral sense of community experience, however community may in any particular instance be defined, while the norms of the administrative courts arise from a certain sociological view of public needs in immediate circumstances of given times and places. Both systems seemed to have developed fine noses for disaster, but for disasters of a different kind. For the exercise of police powers looks to avoid or minimize accidents, while the regular courts look to uphold that sense of law which engages personal responsibility. So the tension between a public order, defined by officialdom's expertise in directing the traffic of ideas, and justice, defined by personal ethics, is but an institutionalized reflection of the ever-present paradox of French constitutional theory which Tocqueville once summed up in these words:

> The nation as a whole has sovereign rights, while the individual [is] kept in strictest tutelage; the former [is] expected to display the sagacity and virtues of a free race, and the latter to behave like an obedient servant.[21]

It is to a commentary on political consequences of this paradox that the final chapter is devoted.

CHAPTER FIVE

The Politics of Law v. Order

> Although it may behoove Socrates and minds of his stamp
> to acquire virtue through reason, the human race would have
> perished long ago if its preservation had depended only on
> the reasoning of its members.
>
> Rousseau, *Discourse on Inequality*

The preceding chapters have shown how the legal system of
contemporary France works in two different and sometimes
opposed ways to regulate freedom of speech. The persistent division of responsibilities between public official and private citizen
enshrined by this system encourages us to look for signs of duality
in the broader framework of the political culture itself. To begin,
let us consider interpretations of an important year in the history of the Fifth Republic, from May 1968 to May 1969. In
the latter part of that year, a charismatic political leader, the
better part of whose domestic political support had been aroused
by his appeals to the *parti de la peur*, resigned, because he was
no longer able to convince his fellowcountrymen that his "certain
idea of France" was worthy of their continued loyalty. And
although as President he had aroused feelings of devotion and
animosity probably unmatched in this century of French politics,
observers thought they noticed a persistent decrease in political
interest among citizens generally during his term of office.
Furthermore, however dramatic he may have wished his
departure to appear, his leadership had already been eclipsed
by the events of May, 1968—that thunderclap out of an apparently clear sky—which caught would-be revolutionaries,

reactionaries, liberals, social scientists, journalists, and the government itself by complete surprise. And when the apparent calm succeeding that sudden storm revealed again the breadth of popular sentiment simply opposed to any rocking of any ship of State, one of the better known of French commentators, Raymond Aron, stated that the principal weakness of France was her inability to conceive of a legitimate government.[1] Are there better examples of the dualities of French civic spirit, of contrasts between appeals to public virtue and private calculation, than these? But phenomena of this sort are so far from new in French political history that they were given virtually classical expression by Tocqueville more than a century ago:

> Ordinarily the French are the most routine-bound of men, but once they are forced out of the rut and leave their homes, they travel to the ends of the earth and engage in the most reckless adventures. Undisciplined by temperament, the Frenchman is always readier to put up with arbitrary rule, however harsh, of an autocrat than with a free, well-ordered government by his fellow citizens, however worthy of respect they be. At one moment he is up in arms against authority and the next we find him serving the powers-that-be with a zeal such as the most servile races never display. So long as no one thinks of resisting, you can lead him on a thread, but once a revolutionary movement is afoot, nothing can restrain him from taking part in it. That is why our rulers are often taken by surprise; they fear the nation either too much or not enough, for though it is never so free that the possibility of enslaving it is ruled out, its spirit can never be broken so completely as to prevent its shaking off the yoke of an oppressive government. . . .

> France alone could have given birth to revolution so sudden, so frantic, and so thoroughgoing, yet so full of unexpected changes of direction, of anomalies and inconsistencies.[2]

And yet even Tocqueville thought these phenomena were based on inexplicable features of the French temperament!

> When I observe France from this angle I find the nation itself far more extraordinary than any of the events of its long history. It hardly seems possible that there can ever have existed any other people so full of contrasts and so extreme in all their doings, so much guided by their emotions and so little by fixed principles, always behaving better, or worse, than one expected of them. . . .Their basic characteristics are so constant that we can recognize the France we know in portraits made of it two or three thousand years ago, and yet so changeful are its moods, so variable its tastes that the nation itself is often quite as much startled as any foreigner at the things it did only a few years before.[3]

French temperament by and of itself may be inexplicable. But the recent events just mentioned, and Tocqueville's observations, both point unmistakably to a certain French unwillingness to settle for a single line of political conduct. The duality of French courts, illustrated in matters of free speech by their formal distinction between the demands of order and law, suggests the possibility of searching for mutual reflections between the legal system on the one hand and political perspectives on the other.

If there is one key to understanding the correspondence of the legal system's duality and that of political perspectives in general, it may well be found in the psychology of dividing responsibilities for the maintenance of order, on the one hand, and for the maintenance of law, on the other. Legal liabilities arise in matters other than speech, of course. But the way freedom of speech is handled is especially indicative of political perspectives, because expressions of ideas in public characteristically involve active and intangible, rather than passive and tangible, duties to the public thing, or to the community. By defining the limits of free speech, a legal system in effect defines the character of political participation, thus giving an authoritative view of what it means to be an active citizen, rather than a mere holder of property or other private rights.

By assigning all policing authority to public officials exclusively, and by holding authors and speakers legally liable only for the maintenance of merely conventional moral views the French legal system in effect does two things. It builds a remarkable barrier between police function and the expression of political ideas, on the one hand, while encouraging a popular feeling that political discourse should essentially involve moral judgments, on the other. As the public official is formally permitted to know ideas only in an external way, in relation to the physical order of his area, so the speaker or writer is freed to present ideas in terms of their intrinsic value.

From the author's or speaker's point of view, indeed, to be held legally liable only to conventional morality, and usually only at the risk of symbolic punishment, is to feel under a moral obligation to be ready to criticize moral conventions in order that ideals of justice may be served.

The system of dual jurisdictions is thus of a piece with the political culture at large, by furthering three of that culture's most obvious characteristics. These are (1) total dependence on official policing mechanisms for the maintenance of the immediate physical order, (2) a broad cynicism with respect to the claims of conventional morality as interpreted by conventional institutions like the courts, and (3) an equally widespread feeling, that moral questions, not the mere maintenance of order, are what law and politics should really be about. The rhetoric of public political discourse in France tends to be generous and abstract, with frequent reference to the ethical values which, held in common, are purported to give France its name and Frenchmen their unique identity. But the rhetoric of private political discourse is altogether different. It consists largely of expression of distrust and cynicism of any political activities, which are commonly taken as means to private power and satisfaction at the expense of the innocent (passive) citizen. And in this chasm between public and private there lives the

State in all its bureaucratic forms, fed not by the respect for its minions but by the feeling that a privatistic order is better than one which would demand once and for all the sacrifice of abstract individuality. For it is only in the exercise of abstract individuality that faith in the myth of true revolution, and of a true liberty, equality, and fraternity, can be nourished. And it is just this faith in the transcendence of history by France herself that makes Frenchmen French.

But why should France feel the need for transcending her own history? Why should contemporary French culture inculcate not only a sense of the difference between actual political practices and an ideal of justice, but go further to inculcate a sense of the perpetual need for such a differentiation?

We need hardly go back to those "ancient portraits" mentioned by Tocqueville to know that one or another form of philosophical dualism has been the hallmark of western philosophy for millenia. That the French political and legal culture should reflect some form of this dualism is therefore perfectly normal. What needs to be asked is what the specifically French forms of the dualism are, and why they have taken such forms. Answers to the latter question must evidently lie in the realm of religious psychology, beyond the scope of this work. But in order to suggest the specific nature of the French dualism the briefest of sketches of such a psychology will have to be suggested here for, as Charles Péguy once wrote, although "politics laughs at mysticism, it is this very mysticism which nourishes politics." The task is in effect to come to grips with the mysticism peculiar to French politics.

All modern constitutional democracies claim to be secular, and all at the same time propose ideals which constitute the basis of what may be called civil religions to their citizens. In times of war these civil religions demand the sacrifice of their votaries—their lives and even their properties—on the altar of national destiny. The question is, therefore, how do modern constitutional democracies, whose routine political life rests relatively unabashedly on a thorough-going utilitarianism, essentially privatistic in its nature, maintain, short of war, in the background, ready for mobilization so to speak, a spirit of patriotism that in all likelihood is the *sine qua non* of national identity as historically and traditionally conceived?

Asked of reflective Americans, such a question usually gives rise to the speculation that our Protestant founders somehow inculcated in our political mores a sort of Old Testament faith in God's special favor. Assuming, in the Protestant manner, a God of will rather than one of reason, we nevertheless believed almost from the first that the New World was the beneficiary of a new ark of the covenant, so that in effect we were building our "City upon a hill." Our alleged freedom from the sins of the Old World and, more recently, our power and prosperity, have been cited as evidence of divine favor. But fundamentally, the American civil religion, like all religions, has gone beyond the search for external evidence, even of economic, technological, and organizational miracles, to elaborate a faith held implicitly and interiorly. And that faith has notably been strong, if perhaps not the strongest, among those elites with the fewest doubts about the relationship of their private wealth and status to the well-being of the nation as idea and ideal. In effect, wealth, status, and conformity to the orthodoxies of American political doctrine sometime seem to be taken as external signs of true belief, at least by their holders.[4] How could it be otherwise, indeed, so long as people (and organizations) of wealth and status are to justify to themselves the pleasurable inequalities they enjoy? Such inequalities do not at all mean that they wish to deny the masses understanding of the mysteries of the faith. But the priesthood is after all more knowledgeable and more *responsible* for salvation than the mass of believers, no matter how devoted the latter may be in their faith.

Whatever the broad validity of the view that the cultures of all advanced industrial nations are essentially Protestant now —that something like the Protestant ethic is as necessary to industrialism as it is to constitutional democracy—it can hardly be argued that French civil spirit rests on the same specific foundation of belief as the American, or that the priesthood of her civic religion expresses itself in the same tones. The very fact that private wealth in France is not merely not flaunted but in fact concealed by enormous ingenuity suggests that even the priesthood itself is of a different character. Nor does the degree of intimacy of private wealth and political power—surely as great, if not indeed greater than in the United States—negate the differences.

These differences can be summed up, it seems to me, in the extraordinary ambivalence of attitude toward politics in contemporary French life, an ambivalence which at one end holds actual political life in cynical contempt and at the other as the potential expression of perfect justice. The contempt seems at first glance to require little explanation; is it not merely an exaggeration of the cynicism increasingly felt in American life about politicians in general? Has it not already been explained by Tocqueville in terms of the fragmentation of modern society?

> In a community in which ties of family, of caste, of class, and craft fraternities no longer exist people are far too much disposed to think exclusively of their own interests, to become self-seekers practicing a narrow individualism and caring nothing for the public good. . . . Since in such communities nothing is stable, each man is haunted by a fear of sinking to a lower social level and by a restless urge to better his condition. And since money has not only become the sole criterion of a man's social status but has also acquired an extreme mobility . . . everybody is feverishly intent on making money or, if already rich, on keeping his wealth intact. Love of gain, a fondness for business careers, the desire to get rich at all costs, a craving for material comforts and easy living quickly become ruling passions. . . . Lowering as they do the national morale, they are despotism's safeguard, since they divert men's attention from public affairs and make them shudder at the mere thought of a revolution. Despotism alone can provide that atmosphere of secrecy which favors crooked dealings and enables the freebooters of finance to make illicit fortunes. Under other forms of government such propensities exist, undoubtedly; under a despotism they

are given free rein. . . . Our quarrel is not about the value of freedom *per se*, but stems from our opinion of our fellow men, high or low as the case may be; indeed, it is no exaggeration to say that a man's admiration for absolute government is proportionate to the contempt he feels for those around him.[5]

If this were all that could be said, if this were the whole truth of modern society, it is hard to see why France should continue to have any existence at all in the minds of her citizens, for they would be able to recognize one another as equal only in servitude. And it is true that much political life seems to reflect such awareness.

But the awareness of this theme is itself a sign that a more fundamental theme exists. And one way of trying to describe this more fundamental theme is to raise the question of the relationship of political activity to history. Like Americans, the French have often thought of themselves as having a cultural mission in the world. But this mission has surely not been to create the "City upon a hill." It has aimed more at providing a message than a model for mankind. And this message is that men are solely responsible for their politics, and that political life must not be treated as a subdiscipline of any other field of endeavor whether natural science or economics, sociology or even theology. This is to say that Reformation thinking, once rejected in its original religious terms, penetrated France in political and philosophical terms instead. That mystical body of Christ which is in Protestant thought constituted by all the true faithful in perfect communion beyond the City of Man and its essentially corrupt institutions, seems to have been transformed in French cultural development into a political idea— a "certain idea of France"—which has been in dispute with the eighteenth century's dry and skeptical utilitarianism ever since the Revolution over the real meaning of "liberty, equality, fraternity."

In this respect French political ideas reflect the ancient Greek ideal of the *polis* as the form of human association which by embracing all the rest is the most human, the highest and the

146

most demanding. But the immediate terms of reference are no longer Greek and mythic. They are, rather, Cartesian and linguistic. Rousseau posed the problem thus:

> Ancient politicians incessantly talked about morals and virtue, those of our time talk only of business and money. One will tell you that in a given country a man is worth the price he would fetch in Algiers; another, following this calculation, will discover some countries where a man is worth nothing and others where he is worth less than nothing. They evaluate men like herds of cattle. According to them a man is worth no more to the State than the value of his domestic consumption.[6]

But if this is true, of what use or value the inevitable restrictions of social living? As Rousseau saw it, the purpose of political association was not to order men according to economic criteria but to turn the individual of the species from a "limited and stupid animal into an intelligent being and a Man," thus "forcing him to be free,"[7] not in terms of his private choices in "domestic consumption" but rather in terms of his essential humanity as contributor to and sharer in collective life.

Thus although all modern western political thought builds more or less from an idea of a social contract, there is nevertheless a fundamental divergence between those forms of the contract which are drawn up in terms of a language and ethics based on private economic calculations and those which are drawn up in terms of a moral conception of public well-being different in kind from the sum of private satisfactions—a sum which its opponents, like Rousseau, regard as logically devoid of cultural, and therefore human, meaning.

The condition of human rights and constitutionalism in contemporary France appears to reflect the conflict so delineated. It found historical expression even within the Revolutionary era, splitting Jacobins and Girondins, "mountain" and "plain." And it finds reflection today in the ambivalent legal treatment accorded freedom of speech. For what is at stake here, philosophically speaking, is precisely the problem faced by French judges who must weigh the legality of illegality of expressions of opinion: are they bound by the principle of strict interpretation to ignore the spirit behind the expression, just as they are bound by the positive meaning of statutory words? Or, on the contrary, does the very nature of their own legal customs require them to look just as much to the spirit of the institutions they are called upon to defend as to that of the expression they are called upon to judge? The evidence of this study points to the latter obligation. And this means that by distinguishing between law and order, legal processes also throw into relief the existence of a specific moral demand on political life that neither physical order nor the conventional morality of law can answer to.

Even before 1789 French intellectual life was very much bound up with the question of national consciousness, extending all the way from matters or personal and class identities—especially of the so-called Third Estate—to that of the identity of the nation as a whole.[8] With the coming of the Revolution, the spirit of this national consciousness was redefined in terms of its formally rational character: for once you mean to leave tradition behind there is not much else to tie to but formal reason. But the political meaning of reason is always ambiguous, because it has to find expression in a language and in other institutions whose past defies logical analysis. Thus in one sense what is rational is only what works at the moment in a pragmatic or experimental sense. But this meaning is certainly not what the French Revolutionaries meant to give it after the overthrow of the monarchy. On the contrary, reason appeared to them to dictate the establishment of a postive political and legal regime whose legitimacy was to be derived wholly from abstract ideas concerning the relationship of the People to the State, and of men to one another. If the Jacobin wing was impelled by strong sentiments in favor of public solidarity based on idolitarized Reason, the Girondins for their part appeared to think of social bodies in terms of place, motion, weight, and extensions, as though constitution-making were an exercise in mechanics. Thus, though the content of the great civil code was eventually drawn substantially from legal practices of pre-Revolutionary times, its form was nevertheless dictated by concepts whose intellectual ancestors were the same as those of Descartes' "primary qualities" of abstract bodies. And therein, with the notion of the indivisible Republic on the one hand, made up of groups and even individuals atomically conceived on the other, was to lie the fissure underlying all future political life.

This is so because the basic notion of the code implied "a place for everything, and everything in its place." But such a principle can make allowance only for private liberty—a liberty defined in terms of a personal freedom to move in any way not legislatively forbidden. As for public liberty, which must be conceived of in terms of deliberate collective action for public purposes, the spirit of the codes is necessarily antithetical. It is only where the codes remain silent that the realm of public liberty may presumably to begin and, this is, therefore, where the contradictory legacy of a politically-minded Cartesianism has its effect.

That legacy poses an essentially chicken-and-egg dilemma: the citizen may share in making the laws, but only after he has been given his political identity and the forms of political motion by the laws. The national consciousness of France makes Frenchmen. But freedom-loving Frenchmen, whose political motives have in part been formed in a cultural past long antedating 1789, are also supposed to make the laws which are to form their own collective self, as well as that of succeeding generations, even though the future may be no more kind to their views than was the Revolution to the views of its predecessors. When helping to draw up the basic rules by which a society shall live and abiding by those rules after they are in force appear to be both logically and psychologically poles apart, how can the politically vital reconciliation be undertaken?

In a society without revolutionary traditions, living more or less comfortably with its past, the mutual interaction of personal self-consciousness and inherited collective identity is easy to live with. We Americans have been doing so every day and every generation; and when we talk about political change we almost always think in incremental terms, on the assumption that the pursuit of knowledge by those inductive means sanctified by our collective past is bound to be valid in the long run.

But a potential tension that is of no great moment in a nonrevolutionary nation presents an insurmountable contradiction in France. For by the French Revolution both citizen and nation alike were promised an absolute right of self-determination. A man's *cogito, ergo sum*, with its ultimate appeal to self-evidence, was necessarily equally essential to a body politic born anew. And self-evidence allows for no deliberation about historical imponderables. Thus the greater the logical force of the new political beginning, the less the individual's chance to define his own consciousness distinct from that decreed by the whole unless—and this underlies the strong currents of both *incivisme* and the revolutionary myth in contemporary France—he does so in opposition to the established institutions and people in power. The French citizen is thus led at one and the same time to reject any responsibility for an order that seems to be imposed upon him without his own will or consent (*je m'en foutisme*), and to profess opinions which believes (and which he half hopes public authorities will believe—as they pretend to) call for a complete reordering of existing society.

Hence a revolutionary theory whose source lay in the conception of a wholly ontological political mind, necessarily produced two radically opposed tendencies in political life. One finds expression in the most "pragmatic" and even cynical possible views, where anyone who favors personal moral autonomy is taken either to be duplicitous or a potential threat to the very foundations of society itself, which can be maintained only by the most thoroughgoing commitment to self-seeking. The other appears unpredictably from time to time in effusions and protestations of good will, and occasionally a very real personal generosity, combined with ragged choruses of "no's" to all authority, indulged in with all the greater enthusiasm because such expressions risk no contamination by utilitarian considerations. Was it perhaps awareness of this that brought Rousseau to comment that reconciling order and liberty was like squaring the circle?

If contemporary French regimes were based on the positive application of the great codes alone, then, we should have in effect something like this: a society governed by the minutest regulations of legally equal individuals, the sum of whose private motives would provide the total force of public motion. Private utility would provide the principal political bond and thus the principal standard of legitimacy.

But consideration of the judicial treatment of freedom of speech shows that the importance of statutory law, great as it may be in French life for reasons both of its revolutionary associations and its utility, is far from occupying the whole constitutional field. That field is shared with two other claims or perspectives, the broad intuitions of each of which we may also discover in the processes of the dual court systems.

One of these, as we have seen, is that of the administrative courts, with their concern for the maintenance of a kind of public order which may go deeper than conscious political life. It is as if the Council of State has come to regard society as a kind of terrain whose surface features may be altered by individual human purposes, but whose unrationalized tendencies must be protected from the inadvertent pushing and hauling of historical events, at least until such time as society intends to change them fundamentally by an act of collective will. In practice this means being prepared to offer procedures both for the public expression of ideas and for the protection of the functional order where the procedures themselves seem likely to break down for local or contingent reasons. But in this balancing of interests the administrative judges attempt to concern themselves exclusively with the appearances of utility and to avoid as much as possible the kind of moral flavor inherent in the sanctions of the criminal law.

As for the ordinary courts, on the other hand, I think we can see in their treatment of the Press Law and related statutes a spirit usually at odds with the positivism of the criminal codes. That is, between the principle of strict interpretation supposed to govern the application of penal statutes and an interpretation of political and social propositions according to their possible tendencies so that they fall under the purview of the statutes, the latter tendency seems to be the more developed. It is perhaps true that the particular statutory vehicle or article or provision of law against which criticisms are judged may vary from time to time and from regime to regime. But the courts' tendency to express judgment of the wrongness of an idea or opinion in cultural terms—in terms of "bad tendency"—rather than by reference to police considerations appears a constant factor.

It may seem, of course, that this tendency is in fact linked with the idea of the strict interpretation of the criminal law, as the term "strict" may certainly be taken to mean logically rigorous rather than simply favorable to the defendant and his liberty. But even if this definition of strictness should lie at the base of much judicial behavior in the regular courts, the practical effort is a standing invitation to governmental authorities to define their own political perspectives through prosecution. An inclination to suppose that every political and social idea forms part of a self-evident pattern consistent with one perspective, but exclusive of all others, is thereby maintained, and it affects all parties, causes, and institutions bearing on free speech. In contradistinction to the subtle intuition of the administrative courts that leads to their emphasis on close definition of the material facts of public order, the intuition of the regular courts therefore emphasizes the cultural reach of ideas. Neither the functional bond of self-interest whose limits are set by the Penal Code, with its carefully graded scale of punishments for the consideration of the prudent individual, nor that of existing communities, each with its own particular, traditional and more or less unconscious perspectives can, in the eyes of the criminal courts, suffice for the maintenance of the national identity of a Republican state.

The criminal code, the civil and commercial codes and administrative law all together do not, in other words, constitute the entire psychological foundation of the national public order. Along with these, even prior to them in a philosophical sense, there must exist a realm of public liberty, of participatory political life, wherein the ideal values behind the positive regime have their being by a perpetual entering into and coming out of the individual identities of French citizens, thus to constitute the only form of social bond which can raise individuals above self-interest and the nation above historical contingencies.[9] Political Cartesianism thus engenders its paradox: because the nation must have the right to recreate its identity at any moment in order to impose its logic on the forces of unthinking history, it must give the same freedom to the self-conscious man, whose activity may well have to be critical in order to be creative. The State's need to punish expression is thus only the other side of the coin of the absolute need for freedom of expression. It is in this context of this paradox that we may attempt to set forth a French theory of freedom of speech.

The importance that French culture has traditionally attributed to public language may be noted in many ways, from the authority of the *Académie française* in matters of definition and usage to the authority of statutory words in the legal system. Rather than assume the temporal possibility of a final correspondence between the empirical world on the one hand, and our social, moral, and intellectual symbols on the other, whereby sensation, thought and action can be united without forcing things, the tendency of modern French culture has been rather to treat separation between mind and sense, between deductive and inductive reasoning, as the unique characteristic of the human animal, at one and the same time his chief claim to glory and its chief source of pain.[10] The legal place of free speech in contemporary France suggests how deep-seated this dualism is, and how it has sharpened the tension between individual and collectivity while increasing their mutual dependence.

In keeping with this tendency *la doctrine*—French juridical commentary—tends to put rights of conscience and expression into a category distinct from other personal rights, such as those of property. The fact that the latter may receive more clear-cut legal recognition from most social institutions, including the courts, does not indicate their superiority to rights of free speech. Quite the contrary. The very fact that property rights can be positively institutionalized suggests that they reflect the wholly conventional factors of social existence. These factors are supported for utility's sake, of course, but not necessarily for justice's. Rights of thought and conscience are philosophically or logically prior to the functional social order because they provide the means whereby social life in its merely conventional forms can support meaning.

Unlike us Americans, with our Bill of Rights, the French have virtually always refused to allow their declarations of rights to be treated as formal legal rules to be read by courts as controlling of legislative acts. Nor is this refusal to give formal legal sanction the Declaration of Rights a bit of cynicism, allowing the citizens to have pretty principles so long as those in power can claim whatever authority they think they need. The apparent separation between constitutional principle and legal practice shows, rather, a deep-seated feeling that something forever stands between formal assumptions and specific circumstances. Specific events are in the realm of history while rights are in the realm of ideas. If the attempt to link them is the ultimate justification for politics, it is nevertheless an activity which can never be completed either progressively or permanently, and least of all by institutions like the courts, with their highly formalized habits of language. For since when has "righteousness been in the law?"

Thus to make a constitution part of the law which judges can interpret, as Americans do, no doubt reflects a desire to regularize the vital task of bringing institutions and justice together. But does such regularization necessarily serve justice? Or does it merely serve the existing order? To make one's constitution the law of the courts may not necessarily raise legal judgments to the level of the constitution. It may merely reduce the constitution to the level of an instrument of power of lawyers and their clients' private interests.

Not only would the ideal of justice be threatened if this happened, but citizens might well develop with respect to it that form of cynicism which claims all justice to be mere illusion. And if this should happen how could even the most functional of orders be maintained? The best the courts can do, in the French view, is to help make life tolerable rather than just in any more than a highly relative sense. "Even when a city is enjoying the profoundest peace, some men must be sitting in judgment of their fellow men. Even at their best, what misery and grief they cause! No human judge can read the conscience of the man before him."[11]

Yet such a view does not mean that men can put justice aside, anymore than they can ignore self-consciousness and the need for identity in a world which had made them, but which they constantly remake. Nor does it mean that current definitions of even a relatively tolerable order will always be valid; they may not even remain consistent with survival. Rather, the limitation serves as a reminder that principles of abstract right receive their due only if one does not pretend that they can be regularly associated with the daily grind. For although this grind is an inevitable part of human existence and cannot be reformed out of the way, its routines can hardly be mistaken for principles of justice. Yet without hope of justice, these routines would be quite meaningless. Hence, both individuals and society need to believe in justice in order that even utilitarian ways of ordinary existence have form and meaning.

Though we may all agree on the desirability of guiding our daily lives on the basis of principle, the means of doing so will vary from one task to another, and from one culture to another. French revolutionary thinking formally rejects the solution of induction from historical experience just because French institutions traditionally accept it. Hence, unlike Americans for whom practice of wordly prudence is based on faith in the universality of inductive methods whereby justice and daily life are progressively related until the time when all minds will have come to reflect the same external order, the French political perspective is permanently at odds with itself. On the one hand it cannot suppose that whether the God-given order is evident to all men or not is from the point of view of utility indifferent, because it cannot see utility as a wholly autonomous matter. On the other hand, it cannot accept utility on a faith that history or progress will ultimately clarify its true meaning, because to do so is to undermine what it takes to have a specifically human consciousness. To suppose that men and events will spontaneously accord in time with a cosmic purpose ultimately explicable in human terms would thus condemn human minds today, and human rights at their very source as well. The separation of man and nature exists precisely because we are aware of the movement of time, of historical accidents, of the gap between morals and survival. To suppose History and Right, expedience and justice to be tending spontaneously toward the same end is in the French view simply a refusal to face the most important fact of existence. This fact is that human life combines two incommensurable things, historical process and individual consciousness. And neither of them alone is sufficient to give meaning to existence and thus order to society.

For if we look to historical processes by themselves for the principles of justice, then untold millions of human beings—indeed all of them—may properly be ground up and discarded by cosmic operations without our being any the wiser. If men could be thought of as having rights at all, they would be merely the rights of the strongest, or the fittest, derivative entirely from contingency—in short, a contradiction in terms.

If, on the other hand, the meaning of life is to be found wholly in one's own brief and immediate experience, then equal and absolute human rights may be abstractly justified without having any social consequences at all. In French experience the forces of history have always proved themselves notoriously disrespectful of individual men and nations. To accept this disrespect without lifting a finger may be suitable for lemmings, but not for men.

As a consequence there is no place for Frenchmen to stand comfortably between a profound cynicism about political and legal institutions and a constant hope for their regeneration. For them human society does not rest solidly on some natural order, nor are politics and positive law but incidental devices for overcoming some inconveniences in the state of nature, as John Locke said. They are, rather, the expression of the most basic of all human enterprises. To be human means to live in full awareness of the human condition, prepared to be quick rather than dead, yet doing one's best to impose some collective values on life.

Such a view suggests trying to deal with politics in the way an artist handles paints and a blank canvas. To transform indeterminate elements into a work of art the painter takes the materials thrust upon him by circumstances and convention in order to transfigure them according to his own vision. If the artist wants to be intelligible even to himself, the historical nature of these materials cannot be ignored. Art cannot neglect the customary tools and conventions of its discipline. It must take the discipline as it has historically developed in order to transform personal vision or intuition into something of sense both to the artist and the public. But the value of the final result will depend on two things—form and content—which are potentially at war with each other. For content is necessarily the product of circumstances. Hence the artist's vision has to be his own.

The essence of both the citizen's and the nation's problem is thus always the same. No matter how many other men—indeed, no matter how many other societies—have expressed their own transcendent visions through refashioning customary materials, the work has always to be done again by every individual, and every conscious political collectivity in every generation, and perhaps at every moment. Successful attempts for the past do of course have some favorable consequences. They provide examples illustrating what must be done, and they change the stock of materials available for the expression of ideas and consciousness at any given time and place. But neither of these consequences is cumulative, because neither solves the problem of anyone else's struggle for meaning. Good techniques and examples are of no use if he who would use them has no vision and no method of his own.

For this reason no single work of art, no individual life, no political regime, is wholly rational in a universally objective sense. Objectivity is necessarily an aspect of accepted techniques, of convention. To live a life of objective rationality is to treat the mind as but a product of influence upon it, and in ethics, of the social influences. To ignore the autonomous, imaginative possibilities of the mind, to deny individual vision, is not to avoid irrationality. It is to embrace it, for it means accepting the past and present without choice, thus denying human rights of thought and expression as constitutional factors.

In the Cartesian perspective, then, the value of the mind is based on its capacity to see through the ordinary world of things in order to transmute them in a realm of universal and abstract meaning. For without such intellectual autonomy we humans would be wholly a part of process. With it we share in being. Language and self-consciousness force upon us the need to create meaning, but only seem to give us the means to respond. Hence, we share in the glory of God and taste the full bitterness of temporality at one and the same time. We cannot have the glory without the bitterness, and Heaven for bid that we should have the latter without the former:

> . . . Even if there were no God, we should always love justice [and] free though we may be from the yoke of religion, we ought never be free from that of equity. This is what made me think justice eternal and not dependent on the conventions of men. If it should so depend, this would be a horrible truth we should have to hide from ourselves.[12]

This view of rights as at one and the same time an *a priori* and political element in human life distinguishes the French theory of free speech decisively from the utilitarian. To base rights on social utility alone is to risk rendering existentially meaningless the discrete lives of individual men who do not accept or contribute to belief in the rationality of nature's processes, as even that apostle of utility, John Stuart Mill, was once driven to admit: "Liberty, as a principle, has no application to any state of things anterior to the time when mankind have become capable of being improved by free and equal discussion."[13] But even those who do so believe are driven inescapably to the conclusion that in reflecting the functional order of the world they add nothing to God's handiwork. What then could be the meaning of freedom? To put individual rights on the seemingly sound basis of utility only ends in depriving liberty of intelligible purpose. Little difference does it make whether law and public opinion be not oppressive of free speech if its only purpose is to reflect processes which began long before man himself appeared on the scene, and must be here long after he disappears from it.[14]

The legal right of free speech in France thus reflects a perspective on the human condition at variance with a characteristically liberal American view. The French perspective does not associate justice with the discovery or maintenance of objective truths. It does not suppose the function of words and ideas to be the reproduction of nature. Language is the tool by which societies create reason. Words and verbal logic are like the materials of the artist's craft: they must be learned and related one to another according to certain conventions, impressed on the mind from earliest childhood. But this teaching of the need for forms is not meant to supplant a man's own search for meaning. On the contrary, it is meant to provide his only manner of escape from a purposeless unself-awareness. The free use of ideas is as necessary to the making of a man in all his humanity as it is to the nation in the making of its own collective consciousness.

What this humanity and this consciousness may be depend, of course, on a philosophical idea for which there are no certain historical criteria. To attempt to apply such criteria to the mind is to act as if it was a thing, which it is not. To submit throughts and the culture expressing them to anything but criteria of form is therefore really an impossible thing to do. The ideas of one mind or of one culture can be judged by others only in a conventional way. And thus temporal justice lies only formally with those who are authoritzed to judge.

Unlike Americans, therefore, Frenchmen do not generally take an optimistic view of life, wherein increases in knowledge and capacity to manipulate physical and social environments mean progress toward transforming the character of human condition. To compensate for the ethical unintelligibility of the empirical order they must give politics a far more lofty role than have Americans, for whom it has characteristically been but one instrumental adjunct to the exploitation of human and physical resources. Imbued to the roots of the subconscious with a metaphysical dualism, the French have taken it for granted that social institutions, as well as individuals, must argue perpetually over the ethical inscrutability of physical existence. And though institutional participation in this argument is assured by the fact that they are users and keepers of language and other materials of meaning, without which the individual with his abstract rights would have no practical means of expressing them, the more sanctified an institution or usage becomes by the passage of time, the less it can have a truly political legitimacy. This is why, as I have earlier indicated,

the only assertion the French feel can be made definitely about the future is that things will not naturally work out for the best if left to themselves.[15]

The French legal system thus has to give reflection of a paradox to two opposed tendencies, whose reconciliation may be attempted only when institutions, including those of the law, give at least minimum scope to a metaphysical conflict. On the one hand, these institutions must respond to the utilitarian and customarily felt needs of existing social interests. On the other, they must give some due to the claims of both a state and individuals whose political being is ultimately justified only on self-evidence, which is discovered in consciousness and mind and not in outward fact. The legal system is thus inevitably engaged in a continuous struggle within itself, a struggle between principles and conventionally defined "felt necessities of the time." It will of necessity forever be pronouncing "melancholy and lamentable judgment", as St. Augustine wrote, on men whose wrong has been to attempt to express a meaning in their own lives thought dangerous to some piece of conventional wisdom designed to conceal the "horrible truth from ourselves." At the same time, the law, like the nation it both defines and regulates, has a necessary stake in permitting individuals to undertake expression of these meanings, since such attempts are necessary to social vitality. To permit them too great freedom, on the other hand, risks undermining some important part of the conventional beliefs on which current order rests. In French tradition law is thus, like humanity itself, caught between process and being.

In the American constitutional system the sense of this conflict is dulled by two major factors. The first is the manifest destinarian's faith that being and process, mind and matter, may eventually be systematically and objectively related. Much of our social life is "rationalized" on this basis, so we do not ordinarily feel the dilemma strongly. But where it cannot be avoided as, for example, in the obvious conflict between abstract right and established custom concerning race relations, then a procedural factor helps to maintain order. This procedure we call federalism, the rationale of which admits at least the momentary validity of more than a single perspective on justice.

Because the French do not accept faith in the first of these factors we should expect to find an especially important "federal" aspect in their courts. And we do. Here again, there is, of course, a profound irony from the Revolutionary view of law.

Unable to suppose that a rational society could arise spontaneously on the basis of its own customs, the Revolutionaries determined to posit justice on a basis of the abstractions they themselves believed self-evident. Their understanding of the history of the *ancien régime* left them convinced that a just public order could result only from conscious effort of public will. Politics itself was thus to be for them the supreme activity, remaking the spirit of France as Le Nôtre remade nature in his famous gardens. The language of politics must set limits to human nature in order to make sense to the human mind what, left to itself, was intelligible only to God's.

Supposing that a logical order required the rules of statutory language to be applied evenly throughout the nation they distributed courts everywhere. No French citizen was to have to go far to find what reason had to say about justice. One appeal only was to be allowed, and that in a district close to home. The Court of Cassation's only function was to review points of law, not matters of fact. Has the result been that equal justice demanded by Republican principle?

Whether it has or not will be a matter of faith alone. For how can one know whether every man receives his just desserts from any legal system? Variety in similar cases tells us little for, as Aristotle once observed, nothing is more unequal than treating unequals equally. In any case, if the generalizations of the law are especially formal, the ways in which they are applied to the particulars of daily social relations must be undertaken by some methods. But statutes themselves provide few directions. Judges must either provide their own methods or fall back on the solutions offered by others. This is to say that positivism in law must involve enormous difficulties at the very point where statutory rules are brought to bear on specific instances because it provides no determinate means for applying the formal language of the statutes except in terms of the customs and conventions of time and place.

Legal positivism in the French mode here shows its Janus faces. On the one side, statutes as universal rules are the formal source of all law. On the other, however, positivism is necessarily as concerned about facts as about rules. And facts arise and have their meaning only in immediate circumstances. Hence decisional law in a positivist framework must have a base in concrete and particular circumstances that no amount or degree of formal centralization of rules and institutions can possibly ignore, for it is only the judges' appreciation of these circumstances that can direct the concrete application of statute. Hence the paradox of legal positivism, which, at the level of universal rules, of legislation, can do anything "except change a man into a woman," as was once said about the English parliament, but which in instant cases must be bound to the "customs of the community" out of which the facts arise, because it is only by the perceptions of the particular community that the moral sense—and hence the guilt or responsibility of the agent—can be defined.

The wide allowance French judges make for local, even corporatist, habits not only confirms the essentially conventional and conservative role of the ordinary courts in the French legal system but points also to the peculiar strengths of localism in France even in recent times.

For if we take law as predictions of what the courts will do in particular cases, we are driven to the conclusion that there are virtually two kinds of constitutional law in France today, defining the individual's relationships to two different kinds of community. And what the citizen's immediate rights of free speech are will be determined by the court's perception of the community involved by his words. For of types of communities there are really but two—that based on will, which is the

162

national community, and that based on interests, which is traditional and local. And the citizen's rights will be judged according to the different constitution of each.

These differences appear to be like those between a natural organic growth and a self-conscious, rationalized work of art. A traditional, local order is very much a product of natural processes. This means

> a heritage of accepted and unquestioned structures, fixed customs and deep-rooted feelings which bring into social life . . . something of the determined physical data of nature, and of the vital unconscious strength proper to vegetative organisms. It is, further, common inherited experience and the moral and intellectual instincts which constitute a kind of empirical, practical wisdom, much deeper and denser and much nearer the hidden complex dynamism of human life than any artificial construction of reason.[16]

But density and profundity of this practical wisdom does not mean that legal regulation of free speech will accordingly be exercised with especial rigor. On the contrary, French jurisprudence of both court systems and especially that of the Council of State, suggests a sense that these traits of traditional communities make them particularly resistant to subversion by abstract ideas. To their strength the observation of Voltaire is particularly applicable:

> Trumpets never gained any battles nor brought down any walls but those of Jericho. . . . Let people read and let them dance; these two amusements will never do the world any harm.[17]

The strength of the national community is of a quite different order, however. Like the self-conscious individual who must identify himself in terms of his vision, the nation must always remeber that a merely functional ordering is insufficient to its real life. Being a work of art, it can be ruined in logic by one wrong brushstroke or line not in keeping with its particular arrangement of forms. As it is the work of self-consciousness, so it may be undone or redone by acts of self-consciousness. Consequently, it cannot afford Voltaire's easygoing skepticism, but must take heed rather of Rousseau's warning.

> Reconsider, then, the importance of your products; and if the works of the most enlightened of our learned men and our best citizens provide us with so little that is useful, tell us what we must think of that crowd of obscure writers and idle men of letters who uselessly consume the substance of the State.
>
> Did I say idle? Would God they really were! Morals would be healthier and society more peaceful. But these vain and futile declaimers go everywhere armed with their deadly paradoxes, undermining the foundations of faith, and annihilating virtue. They smile disdainfully at the old-fashioned words of fatherland and religion, and devote their talents to destroying and debasing all that is sacred among men. Not that at bottom they hate either virtue or our dogmas; they are enemies of public opinion, and to bring them to foot of the altars it would suffice to send them among atheists. O passion to gain distinction, of what are you not capable?[18]

Now inasmuch as French experience not only suggests the possibility of a renewal of vision, but provides a perspective on political life in which this renewal is demanded, French national politics risks at any moment being confronted with a need to know whether this or that vision of renewal is the right one. Since scanning the physical universe for conclusive signs of objective human justice is not believed fruitful, we are left only with an immediately practical criterion: that vision which succeeds in imposing itself is the legitimate one. Justice, like language itself, is of human creation, and Montesquieu's horrible truth stares France in the face. The Third and Fourth Republics could not stand it. And even now the Fifth is tending toward the same uncertainty.

The immediate failure of the parliamentary regimes arose

from the fact that their most politically articulate figures claimed to believe the People sovereign. If Louis XIV could say "*l'Etat, c'est moi!*" why could not the People say it too, and with more reason? But popular sovereignty is institutionally workable only if you are willing to discover the People's will in the compromises of many varied and even unrelated conflicts of interest. Law then becomes an expression of the procedures which make compromise possible, adding obligatory form to the substance of the compromises reached. Such law *is* then found, and not created. And it is found by many kinds of social institutions, each doing its own work in its own particular way. Legislators, presidents, judges, administrators, mayors, and representatives of every kind of social interest, all contribute their bit. And such law is commonly taken in Anglo-American political life as an acceptable approximation of the public interest and of justice in its immediate state.

A practicable theory of popular sovereignity must therefore be willing to assume law to be reflections, distilled and clarified by institutional techniques, of many contending social forces. Institutions are by definition mirrors to various segments of the People in turn, reflecting what each sees as best as it can according to its own methods. But this is precisely the conception of law that the French Revolutionary ideal has formally rejected. In that tradition, law and politics have to be creative, reflecting not the infinitely complex and morally incoherent situation of historical men but a pure vision of public will. A constitution, then, must by definition be a matter of collective consciousness, not merely of the play of social forces wherein each seeks his private interests as best he may.

Under these circumstances conflict between citizen and State can be minimized only if the two take turns at elaborating their respective visions of justice. From the point of view of free speech the notable feature of the parliamentary system was that it proved largely incapable of stating a national vision of its own. The People collectively were unable to speak with one voice, could not undertake those creative acts which are inherent in French political expectations. As a knowledgeable observer of the Third Republic once noted,

> Parliamentary government does not consist in having ideas
> and applying them under the control of the Chambers, but
> in finding out the ideas of the majority, which for the better
> part of the time do not exist, and giving an appearance to
> this nonexistence.[19]

The field was thus left open to individuals and private association to run in any direction they would. The result was flourish-
ing, highly individualized, fruitless, and occasionally violent debate. It necessarily left the courts of a putatively positivist legal
system in a difficult position where the national community was
at issue.

For having been trained to believe that the will of the People
was law they found themselves at a loss to know what that will
intended. Legislation showed more traces of compromise among
many interests than of clear concepts and intentions. Could the
judges make up for the lack by their own professional techniques?

If they had been bred only in the tradition of private law and
the ancient *droit coûtumier* they might perhaps have attempted
to realize syntheses out of both legislative and social trends and
conflicts. But the revolutionary thrust made judicial analysis and
synthesis of legislative and social trends strictly secondary to
legislation as the source of law, if not actually taboo. And the
organization of the courts made practically impossible sufficient enterprise to permit self-conscious precedent-making, even
if Revolutionary ideas had not interfered. Hence the response of
the courts to parliamentary incoherence was to search for some
secondary source of authoritative will. The highly developed
sense of the particularity of each case characteristic of the jurisprudence of the Council of State, combined with the inherited
sense of its members' natural superiority to the common run of
mortals, made it possible for the administrative law judges to act
rather in the manner of the guardians of Plato's *Republic*—men
with a rationality so exquisitely refined that reference to written
law was quite superfluous. Their confidence was in any event
relative to their very limited function of defining police powers,
which in their own view concerned only the outward appearance

166

of physical order, and not at all the great ethical vision essential to the nation as a whole.

In light of the essential political need for such vision, the task of the regular courts, has, in contrast, been hopeless. In their responses to particular threats to the conventional moral order they have more often than not seemed to reflect a characteristic French attitude to the effect that any and all symbols of public authority must be cosseted and proclaimed admirable to the populace lest all order collapse. In terms of the legal practices of the Third and Fourth Republics, the prime symbol of authority, given the instability of parliamentary governments, was the army. It is not hard to see why. For in addition to the patriotic bloodletting of the first World War, the army stood in the conflicting perspectives of both Right and Left as something of supreme value. A man could admire the symbolism of military authority whether he held with authority over democrary or with the nation in arms at the barricades. Thus have threats to military discipline and morale been regularly discovered by public prosecutors, and about as often punished by the ordinary courts throughout the twentieth century. In the face of the parliamentary fiasco, what other ideal than that the army could have given meaning to the law? Military life involved all those spiritual characteristics supposed vital to national existence. Soldiers applied acts of will to unpredictable circumstances and depended on their collective consciousness to pull them through. Furthermore, the Army was always on guard against ever threatening disasters. It was thus essentially related not merely to the triumphs and tragedies of the previous centuries but to the broadest experience of the culture. For it offered the means by which these triumphs and tragedies might be transformed into a national vision around which the unity of the French people could again be identified. Hence, even as Article 25 of the Press Law contained neither of the conditions of Articles 23 and 24 concerning effects and directness, so has it come to bear a burden of political purposes surely greater then any which its legislative authors could have intended for it in 1881.

Since 1958, and at least until May, 1968, the reestablishment of the authority of the State in the person of Charles de Gaulle, along with the uncertain loyalty of the Army in the final years of the Algerian agony, helped to make punishment of offenses to the President of the Republic (Article 26) the same kind of legal instrument of symbolic authority that Article 25 had been under the previous regimes.

But of course no single legal provision is capable of carrying such a burden by itself. Under the Third and Fourth Republics the best the courts could do was to employ such means to record their own distress in the face of the threats of national dissolution, perhaps in the hope that the public would be reminded that the law could keep things in their place only if a political will first defined that place. There is in all those old repressive decisions the sound of self-conscious political class talking to itself, trying to keep up its own courage in the face not only of difficult external conditions but even more of moral concerns to which genuinely political responses were simply not forthcoming.

Such considerations suggest that the courts have not escaped from the general malaise characteristic of the parliamentary regimes. These regimes failed to provide the one element vital to unquestioned acceptance of the positivists' perspective. This element is a broadly accepted standard by which statutory rules —the "will of the State"—can be interpreted and applied. It is true that the courts did elaborate a set of methods and perspectives by which the civil code was adapted to modern industrialism.[20] But such methods were in almost complete default with respect to individual rights wherever these rights touched on public life. Hence for freedom of speech the courts had to turn elsewhere than to codes and statutes for standards of interpretation.

Yet in attempting to "find" the law themselves, the French judiciary did not move toward a kind of balance of power view of constitutionalism. Even as developed by the administrative courts, the "general principles of the law" show as clearly as the Revolutionary outlook itself that philosophical dualism is still fundamental. For these principles are spoken of as essential absolutes demanding constant reconciliation with events.[21]

Thus, just as French legal positivism is not based on the view that experimentation within a flexible constitutional framework leads to a just society, so these judge-made "general principles" do not reflect the characteristic American view that law should stand for a progressive balance among well-defined social interests. The French legal outlook, like French politics, is inherently ideological because it is part and parcel of a tradition which supposes the need to impose order on collective events, rather than to discover it therein. But if the order to be imposed is neither God nor nature-given, how is one to know whether any particular man-made form of order is legitimate?

The difficulty of answering this question may help to account for that *incivisme* so frequently remarked upon by both Frenchmen and foreigners alike. Often a kind of hidden, personal delinquency, sometimes a peer group delinquency, it reflects both a tendency to think of oneself as a subject rather than as a citizen *and* a resentment at not sharing equally in the creation of a political will. Hence the grudging obedience only to those rules which are effectively enforced.

And the ambiguity of the response of public authorities to *incivisme* is as revealing as the phenomenon itself. Because it reflects a weakness of social solidarity, authorities know that those who display it can always be led by appeals to their self-interest and are thus more dependable subjects than those who are susceptible to the appeals of idealism.[22] Even in the courtroom itself the authority of the judge seems to come more from his place in a bureaucratic hierarchy than from any special capacity to interpret statutory words. For what Frenchman claiming a right to free speech could possibly admit that another's use of his language must inherently be more right than his own? The power to inflict sanctions is really the *sine qua non* of French authority. Where that power is not regarded as certain, authority will be flouted.

So often, therefore, regular authority in France is associated with control of those forces which control pain and pleasure. But like all utilitarianism, the French variety has its own standard by which pain and pleasure are defined. If American utilitarianism thinks vaguely in terms of increasing the number of goods as the best way of contributing to the greatest good of the greatest number, the French view is rather more negative. Public authority is materially justified by its capacity to stave off disasters.

This being the situation, and the most fruitful source of pain being so frequently the quirks of history, authority requires most of all the gift of historical prophecy. This gift in a political leader inspires confidence, because it appears to offer the best hope of reducing the occasion for pain to a minimum.

But that the French constitution in its most formal aspect must therefore fall into the category of periodical literature, as the old joke has it, cannot be invoked as showing the weakness of human rights in France. The very opposite is more likely true: even at the most improbable times, stability may be sacrificed so that we may be reminded that justice and human rights can be found only in voluntary collective action. There being no institutional method by which this world may be linked to justice, constitutions must inevitably be as periodical as the public moods of faith and fear.

The legal order in France appears consequently to incorporate three distinct elements. Of these the least certain in terms of judicial concern is the written constitution itself. It is of the very nature of written constitutions that they are *ad hoc* creations, good for "one trip in one direction only." When history changes the conditions it is only discretion to change one's constitution as well.

Far more stable and influential in the day-to-day operation of the legal system is the combination of statutory law and judicial decision. Though judicial fashions in the interpretation of law modify this element from time to time, it nevertheless seems to come as close to immortality as the French view of institutions will allow. Words set down in orderly fashion, and applied in keeping with the circumstances identifying traditional communities of both occupational and geographical kind, are clearly regarded as an immediate part of continuing moral order.

Binding these two elements together, necessary by virtue of providing the factors which make government at once both possible and subject to overthrow, are freedom of conscience and freedom of speech. Because these freedoms are the only means by which the factor of collective will can express itself, they are equally the only source of legitimacy and meaning in political associations. It is for this reason that of all political forms, only the constituent assembly can come close to the French idea of the spirit of the law.

The matter of political stability in France hence runs deeper than the obvious conflicts of political conceptions her history makes familiar. Unable to believe that the abyss between mind and matter can ultimately be overcome through evolution, organization, or social process, convinced of the personal nature of human dilemma, her citizens may give successive regimes very different amounts of power but rarely either enduring or unlimited confidence. If they are thereby a disappointment to admirers of democratic stability, they nevertheless do not provide soil suitable for despotic cultivation either.

For depotism can hardly send down deep roots among a people whose cultural pessimism is grounded in an awareness of the ironies of self-awareness. A sense of the limitations of ideas is counterbalanced by as strong a sense of the human inadequacy of treating the mind as merely a tool for holding a hostile environment in check. It is surely more than coincidence that a contemporary Frenchmen, Albert Camus, came to retell the story of Sysyphus to express this view of the human condition. Sysyphus has to act out his own task even though he knows that the closer he approaches its accomplishment the sooner his efforts will come to nothing. Fully aware of the irony of his power he nevertheless proceeds with his task in order to impose a purpose on his existence, thereby placing himself temporarily beyond the reach of fate's inscrutability. The stone is his happiness. What counts is not that he succeed in a hopeless task, but that he live it out to the end by his own act of will. Personal courage and sympathy for other humans, and the desire to communicate with them, are thus the enduring political virtues because only they point the way to this kind of meaning. From this perspective the established conventions of life—political, legal, social—must all be judged failing by the mere fact of their evident existence.

Such a perspective is clearly a hard one to live with. So hard, indeed, that it may help account for what can only be described as the apparent sign of relief with which in 1958 the French let parliamentarianism collapse. Whatever may have been its economic achievements, they manifestly failed to compensate for its manifold moral and psychological failure. It was specifically in the matter of developing and applying an appropriate vision of history that the parliamentary system showed its incompetence most appallingly. For a while the Third Republic had its blood-bespattered *union sacreê*. But the Fourth Republic's only vision was of a reformed colonial empire, and this at the very moment when empires were rapidly becoming impossible to maintain.

The movement toward a united Europe, on the other hand, apparently does not fulfill the criterion of a vision at all, probably because such successes as it may be thought to have had are largely of an economic order. European planning has shown unmistakable signs of improvisation and compromise, and of using private tendencies toward cartelization to overcome obstacles to freer trade. European unification is thus seen as a characteristic element of the functional aspects of existence, especially as the specifically political institutions for the furtherance of the cause have tended to wither on the vine as the administrative ones have developed. For all its contributions to that cause then, the Fourth Republic was unable to find moral support among its own public in its final crisis.

The relative affluence of France today has lately been scanned by social scientists for signs that the traditionally ideological character of her political life is at last dying out. It is sometimes argued that the forces which have created the new prosperity in part reflect and in part create new popular values resembling those of American society. This shift in values, it is sometimes said, will finally make possible stable political institutions, order and liberty, a regime in which economic growth allows politics to become but the means of dealing with otherwise unregulated conflicts of private interest.

Whatever may be the case elsewhere in the industrial world, the shadow de Gaulle still casts on France should give pause to those who predict such changes with confidence. No doubt his presidency did encourage French energies to flow in private economic ways. By arrogating the political realm—the realm of ideas, the realm of the national will—to himself, he seemed to remove what had proved an onerous and frustrating burden to the public at large. Especially after 1962 the Fifth Republic allowed all those many Frenchmen who wanted respite from the metaphysical struggle of defining the national conscious-ness to devote their energies largely to the private activities which butter their bread and fuel their cars. With the help of an able group of technocrats coordinating the economic side of things, the President himself could appear to spend his notable spirit toward raising France above what the forces of contem-porary world affairs would ordinarily allow her.

It was in this division of labor between Government and Peo-ple that the essential role of de Gaulle must be found. He seemed to provide a political vision of France rising above what her catalogued resources would have allowed her. Even those who opposed him seemed often to object rather to the substance of his vision than to its form. And thus in an age when ideologies are supposed to be dead or dying, de Gaulle made much of a feeling for history far beyond the usual grasp of technicians, ad-ministrators, lawyers, or parliamentary politicians.[23]

That he often used his authority outside the limits of the con-stitution he himself established indicated his own awareness of its real source. Institutionalization of his vision would have been a contradiction in terms, as if one attempted to treat an ordered consciousness as the spontaneous work of history. So long as de Gaulle was President, the constitution of the Fifth Republic therefore remained what de Gaulle's outlook required. And by and large most Frenchmen were willing to accept that view, if only for the passive satisfaction of believing, in their metaphysi-cal weariness, that they were ruled by a public figure who could temporarily outwit circumstances.

The source of de Gaulle's authority was therefore neither legal nor constitutional in the American sense of those terms. Yet it had its formal aspect even so, because it responded to the cultur-al demand for a will capable of imposing itself on the collective life of the nation. If the events of 1968 finally showed his method to be as vulnerable to the tides of history as earlier ones, we may

173

first guess that the cause sprang more from certain economic weaknesses than from considerations of political justice. After all, do not private men with their ordinary ways of looking at things have a dominant claim in this age?

But is it not true that the source of the Fifth Republic's troubles of those years lay as much in the General's perspective on politics than in any functional economic imbalances that occurred during his presidency? The very force of de Gaulle's idea of France in foreign affairs meant that domestic arrangements were left largely to those elements which could organize and produce effectively. Yet the idea of the grandeur of France is at least as closely tied with the ideas of *liberté*, *egalité*, *fraternité* as it is with international standing and gold deposits. Thus the technocracy, so manifestly an important part of recent government, and the social and economic interests of the upper middle class, from which the technocracy itself spring, were allowed to take precedence over the Revolutionary sense of justice which, if perhaps dulled in the age of struggle for affluence, had yet to desert Frenchmen altogether. In reviving the revolutionary conception of the State as a product of its own self-consciousness de Gaulle proved once again that no human enterprise can escape its own irony. For all his apparent attempts to avoid that kind which might have been associated with adhering to the constraints of his own regime, those typical New Year's Day speeches, so generously larded with statistical reminders that the French had never enjoyed so much peace and prosperity, must finally have touched an old nerve sensitive to the idea of a public good distinct from private affluence. And thus his skill, which once seemed to many as paying due respect to both law and order, came in the glare of 1968 to be seen as far more committed to the latter than to the former.

Amibivalent public reactions during and since that year remind us that many Frenchmen once again feel uneasily called to enter the troublesome and troubled world of direct politics, to engage themselves personally in efforts to reestablish purposes for public life which de Gaulle's personality, by attraction for some, by opposition for others, had made temporarily superfluous. As the latest Presidential elections suggest, the General has begun to appear to many Frenchmen no longer as a man standing above history, but rather as only one of many landmarks, and thus a challenge to their own force of mind and will.

Insofar as Gaullism has entered into political institutions it has become only a part of the merely conventional existence. Memories of the man's example will live on, though, converted by the most basic factors in French culture into one of those historical myths which, like that of May 1968 itself, will contribute to the shaping of future political vision. But as these myths take their place in the political usages of the succeeding generation there will be those who inveigh, as Frenchmen always have, against the mystification of politics, claiming that any existing order is always its own justification. And thus will France continue to be torn between those two points of view Rousseau long ago characterized as the poles of politics, from which the only surcease are *incivisme*, charismatic leadership, and ritual rebellion. For, as Rouseau wrote, the problem of the signs by which we may know whether a people is well or badly governed, can never be resolved,

> each man [wishing] to answer the question in his own way. The subject boasts of public law and order, the citizen of the freedom enjoyed by the individual. The first prefers the security of property, the second that of the person. The first will maintain that the harshest government is the best, the second the gentlest. The first wants to see crime punished, the second to make crime impossible. The first thinks it a fine thing that a country should be feared by its neighbours, the second prefers that they should ignore it. The first is happy when money circulates, the second demands bread for the people.

And Rousseau concluded:

> Even if agreement be reached on these and similar points, are we any nearer to an answer? There is no scale by which moral qualities can be assessed.[24]

175

Perhaps there is none. But the legal processes described in this work, by their positivism which is at once pragmatic and conventional in practice, yet idealist in pretension, encourage a sense among Frenchmen that they will sooner or later be called upon to weigh moral qualities nevertheless. And this expectation, partly dreaded, partly hoped for, reminds them that their willingness to disagree over how the weighing is to be done is just what makes them French, and just what lends their forms both of government and of contestation such legitimacy as they will ever have.

Notes

Notes to the Preface

1. Cf. H. L. A. Hart, *The Concept of Law*, 1961, London, 191, for one measure of the phrase "mutual forbearance".

2. Tocqueville, *Democracy in America*, Heffner ed. and abrdg., 1956, New York and Toronto, 117 (Part I, ch. 2 in the original).

3. Ibid., 48.

4. "Usefulness" may be defined negatively as Hegel does, for example, when he says that evil expressions may often strengthen public conviction in favor of sound opinion. *The Philosophy of Law*, § 319.

5. *Schenck v. United States*, 249 U.S. 47, 52 (1919).

6. Generally in French law, as in American, liability may be engaged in minor criminal offenses and in most civil ones, without proof of scienter. However, where the right to reparations of plaintiffs in defamation cases is determined in connection with criminal proceedings, as may often occur in France, discovery of *scienter* is likely to be a factor in determining the amount of reparation.

7. *Leviathan*, 1958, Indianapolis and New York, 24. (Introduction to Part I).

8. "Bentham" in G. Himmelfarb ed., *Essays in Politics and Culture by John Stuart* Mill, 1963, Garden City, 102.

Notes to Chapter One

1. McCulloch v. Maryland, 4 Wheaton 316 (1819).

2. This account and the documents are drawn from the *conclusions* (summing-up) of *Commissaire du gouvernement* Michel: C. E. May 19, 1933, *Benjamin*, D. P. 1933. 3. 54. The citation stands for C(onseil d') E(tat), judgment handed down on May 19, 1933, plaintiff's name, title of court report, in this case, D(alloz) P(ériodique), volume for 1933, section 3, which contains reports of the administrative courts, the instant case beginning on p. 54. Relative to the Benjamin case, see also C. E. February 5, 1937, *Bijadoux et al*, D. 1938. 3. 19, *concl.* Lagrange, where a decision of the Prefect, supported by the Minister of the Interior, to prohibit a public banquet organized by a proto-fascist group that had been declared illegal by the so-called Loi Maurras of January 10, 1936, was overturned by similar reasoning.

3. Rather like troubadours of another age, and before radio made them obsolete, *hommes de lettres* like Banjamin went from town to town of the provinces to provide winter entertainment and instruction to those elements of the provincial bourgeoisie and gentry whose tastes and incomes made the world of Paris too brilliant, daring, and expensive. Benjamin had been invited to give two lectures in a series of eight that Nevers' *syndicat d'initiative* had organized, and called, perhaps with some exaggeration, *galas littéraires*. The combined title for Benjamin's part was "Sacha Guitry and Courteline: Two Comic Authors."

4. A *syndicat d'initiative* performs some of the same tasks as an American chamber of commerce but, unlike the latter, is a subsidized agency of municipal government.

5. More dedicated to violent words than violent deeds, *Action française* constituted a political movement of the extreme Right of French politics during the first half of the 20th century. Founded in reaction against the separation of Church and State and the very relative triumph of the *dreyfusards*, its major spokesman from 1905 to 1950 was Charles Maurras. His doctrines of "integral nationalism," pseudoclericalism, psuedomonarchism, anti-semitism, and anti-parliamentarianism led to the rather archaic distinction of the 1920s of having his literary works and newspaper placed on the Vatican's *Index* because of the Papacy's decision then to reach an accomodation with the Third Republic. As a movement, *Action française* was at its greatest strength prior to World War I and again in the '30s, and its activities were a major reflection, though hardly the major cause, of the political demoralization of the Republic that led to Vichy. Maurras and his followers became apologists for the Vichy regime and many were later sentenced to prison by Liberation courts. Although *Action française* virtually ceased to exist as an effective movement after World War II, Maurras and others began a new

journal of the same political disposition called *Aspects de la France et du Monde* during the Fourth Republic. In his study *Democracy in France*, 4th ed., New York, 1964 at 142, David Thomson remarks that "between 1905 and 1925, the majority of men who became French bishops came from schools, circles and social spheres where the political outlook of the *Action française* prevailed . . . There is . . . a direct link between the bitterness of the Dreyfus affair and the feuds of the inter-war years which helped to kill the Republic in 1940. . . ."

Among Banjamin's literary works there was much political writing. In 1930 he published *Clemenceau dans la retraite*, the major theme of which was Clemenceau's loss of faith in democracy and in the Republic: "Hope? Impossible. How can I go on hoping when I no longer believe in that which aroused me, namely, democracy?" Cited in Hannah Arendt, *The Origins of Totalitarianism*, Cleveland, 1958, 93, n. 9.

6. Cited in Daniel J. Boorstin, *The Mysterious Science of the Law*, Boston, 1958, 165-66. *Commentaries*, IV. 151H.

7. In a subsequent case for damages the Council of State declared: "The prohibition of public meetings by the mayor may constitute a serious fault of such a nature as to engage the liability of the commune." C. E. April 3, 1936, *Benjamin*, D. 36. 3. 31/

8. On the function of the *commissaire du gouvernement* in the judicial operations of the Council of State see C. J. Hamson, *Executive Discretion and Judicial Control*, London, 1954, 79-81. Also Charles Freedeman, *The Council of State in Modern France*, New York, 1961, 189-90, and Tony Sauwel, "Les origines des Commissaires du gouvernement auprès du Conseil d'Etat statuant en contentieux," *Revue du droit public* (RDP) LXV, 1949. 5. The *commissaire du gouvernement* does not necessarily take the State's case, but is free, in Hamson's words, to represent the "conscience" of the court. In rendering judgment, the Council of State is by no means obilged to adopt either his arguments or his conclusion, although it often does.

9. David Thomson, *Democracy in France since 1870*, 4th ed., New York and London, 1964, 59.

10. Quoted in Eugene Blum, *La Déclaration des droits de l'homme et du citoyen*, Paris, 1902, 267.

11. T. E. Emerson, "Toward a General Theory of the First Amendment," 72 *Yale Law Journal* 5, April 1963, 889. See also *Elliot's Debates on the Constitution*, 2nd ed. 1866, 569, cited by John H. Kelly, "Criminal Libel and Free Speech," 6 *Kansas Law Review* 305, 313 (1958).

12. For a comment on the utilitarian justification of free speech in American constitutional decisions see Charles Fairman, *American Constitutional Decisions*, New York, 1948, 409-10. A major statement of this kind is Holmes' dissent in Abramns v. United States, 250 U. S.

616 (1919). But the resemblance to John Stuart Mill's view in *On Liberty* is surely more apparent than real. See also Roberts' dissent in Terminiello v. Chicago, 337 U. S. 1 (1949).

13. Schenck v United States, 249 U. S. 47 (1919).

14. The weakness of Holmes' argument in favor of a "clear and present danger" approach as a means of determining guilt or innocence is revealed in his Abrams' dissent. There he wrote that "we should be eternally vigilant against attempt to check expression of opinions that we loathe and believe to be fraught with death, unless they so imminently threaten immediate interference with the lawful and pressing purposes of the law that an immediate check is necessary to save the country." Given the slowness of all legal proceedings in matters of constitutional importance, it is hard to see how judicial activities could ever constitute 'an immediate check' capable of saving a country. Only censorship under police powers could conceivably operate such a check. Nor is it clear, on the moral side of the question, why an individual should be obliged under threat of criminal sanction not to take advantage of circumstances most favorable to the propagation of his views. Cf. Walter F. Berns, *Freedom, Virtue, and the First Amendment*, Baton Rouge, 1957, 49-57. Whether a "clear and present danger" test has, or has ever had, an operative effect in American law is beside the point I am making here. The fact that it has been raised and discussed seriously as a factor of decision in *criminal* law is what distinguishes American attitudes from French in the matter.

15. C. E. November 23, 1951, *Société nouvelle d'imprimerie*, RDP. 1951. 1105.

16. C. E. February 23, 1966, *Société Franco-London et Société des films Gibé*. J. C. P. (*Juris-Classeur Périodique*). 1966. II. 14608.

17. The reference is to C. E. December 18, 1959, *Societe "Les films Lutétia"* S(Sirey). 1960. 94 *concl*. Mayras, a case in which the Council of State upheld the banning of several movies by the Mayor of Nice, who acted under pressures from diverse local groups that found the censorship of the Ministry of Commerce and Industry altogether too liberal for their various tastes. Mayors can appropriately exercise their police powers, according to this decision, with respect to films whose "projection is likely to bring about serious disturbances or to be, by reason of the immoral character of said film and local circumstances, prejudicial to the public order." See Long, Weil, Braibant, *Les grands arrêts de la jurisprudence administrative*, Paris, 1962, 472-77 for commentary.

18. Cf. H. L. A. Hart, *The Concept of Law*, London, 1961, 193-5 especially.

19. This is natural in any country where the class of private lawyers has so much importance as in France. In this connection, note the Fifth Republic's repeated attempts to reform and codify the rules of legal ethics.

20. See, for example, Roger Pinto, *La Liberté d'opinion et d'information,* Paris, 1955. For the development of French administrative practice and law in the context of historical institutions see P.-F. Benoit, *Le Droit administratif,* Paris, 1968, 4-5 and the literature cited in the notes thereto. Also, note Rousseau's significant comment in *Social Contract,* Book III, Chapter 2, on the necessity of a governmental will as distinct from the General Will.

Notes to Chapter Two

1. Flaubert, *Sentimental Education* (1869) R. Baldick, tr. Hammondsworth, 1964, 264, includes a scene in which the lawyer Deslauriers, at a party late in 1847 where the talk turns to politics, takes out his notebook and reads:

> Since the 'best of republics' [i.e. the July monarchy] was established, we have had 1,229 prosecutions of the press, as the result of which our journalists have been sentenced to 3,141 years' imprisonment and fined the trifling sum of 7,110,500 francs. It makes a pretty story, doesn't it?

Cf. Irene Collins, *The Government and the Newspaper Press in France, 1814-1881,* London, 1959, 76-77, 99.

2. See Gordon Wright, *France in Modern Times, 1760 to the Present,* Chicago, 1962, 296-324, 343-326 *Passim.* The fundamentally constitutional legislation of the first three decades includes, besides the Press Law, the following: establishment of free, public primary education June 16-17, 1881, with obligatory attendance coming on March 28-29, 1882; the law of association, July 1-2, 1901; separation of Church and State, December 9, 1905; the law governing public meetings, March 28, 1907. This list probably ought to include also the law of municipal organization April 5, 1884, the intention of which was to strengthen local government and effect a degree of administrative decentralization. In the realm of purely judicial rules, that of 1897 recognizing the right to defense counsel in all criminal cases, from the first appearance of the defendant before the examining magistrate (*juge d'instruction*) through

to the end of the appeals process, is also obviously of constitutional importance.

3. Christopher Plantin, *Bonheur de ce monde* (Happiness of This World) quoted in Emile Servan-Schreiber, *Alors raconte!*, Paris, 1967, 10:
> To have a comfortable house, neat and pretty,
> A garden lined with sweet smelling trees
> Some fruits, good wine, little fuss, few children;
> To act in moderation on all matters.
> To say one's rosary while cultivating one's grapes. . . .
> And quietly wait at home for death.

4. Laurence Wylie, "Change at the Grass Roots", in Hoffmann and others *In Search of France*, Cambridge (Mass.) 1963, 204.

5. Wright, *France in Modern Times*, 300.

6. Statutory texts are drawn here from Dalloz, *Code Pénal annoté d'après la doctrine et la jurisprudence avec renvois aux publications Dalloz* Paris, 1962. The last official publication of the penal code dates from 1832.

7. Rapporteur Lisbonne, *Journal Officiel, Débats, Chambre*, session ordinaire 1881, sitting of January 24, 34.

8. See Irene Collins, *Government and Newspaper Press*, 141-163.

9. Alain-Targé, *J.O.*, *Déb.*, *Ch.*, January 28, 1881, 70-71.

10. Ibid., January 30, 1881, 74.

11. The term *droit commun* in French means generally that law applicable to all citizens without regard to their social, economic, or political functions, law, that is, not based on classification of this sort. In practice the term is generally used to refer to the criminal and civil codes. The Press Law, for example, although technically an appendix to the criminal code has phrases in it the operation of which implies classifications of people as, say, editors, publishers, printers, hawkers, authors, etc., and by distinguishing between the degrees of liability to be incurred by each class thereby removes itself from the category of the *droit commun*.

12. *J.O.*, *Déb.*, *Ch.*, January 26, 1881, 61.

13. *Délits d'opinion*, literally "offenses of opinion", characterized earlier laws allowing prosecution for mere statements of personal view unaccompanied by any statement of purpose or advocacy. Such offenses were usually enumerated as follows:
> (1). Incitement to disobey the law;
> (2). Libel of public or religious morality;
> (3). Libel of religions recognized by the state;

(4). Attack against liberty of worship;

(5). Attack against the Constitution;

(6). Incitement to hate or distrust of the Government;

(7). Apology for acts defined as crimes or offenses by law;

(8). Faithlessness or bad faith in reporting parliamentary debates, or hearings of courts and tribunals.

Cf. quote of the Radical Eugène Pelletan in Collins, *Government and Newspaper Press*, 182, on abandonment of *délits d'opinions*.

14. Ibid., 57.

15. Augiel, ibid., January 28, 1881, 68.

16. Painlevy, ibid., January 30, 1881, 80.

17. Augiel, ibid., January 24, 1881, 38.

18. Ibid.

19. Ibid., 66-68.

21. *J.O.*, *Déb.*, *Ch.*, January 24, 1881, 34; January 26, 61.

22. Cunéo d'Ornano, ibid., January 24, 1881, 36.

23. Irene Collins, *Government and Newspaper Press*, 181-183. Also Roger Pinto, *La Liberté d'opinion et d'information*, Paris 1955, 45.

24. *J.O.*, *Déb.*, *Ch.*, January 30, 1881, Gatineau, 83.

25. It is to be recalled that the right of a defendant to counsel had not yet been recognized as a "general principle of the law", so that deprivation of a jury trial might well have had more consequences than loss of a hearing by one's peers. On the other hand, given the kind of people likely to be chosen for jury duty, a genuine anarchist certainly had no more to fear from a panel of judges than from such representatives of the public.

26. The greatest systematic persecution for opinions and beliefs before the First World War was undertaken in connection with the separation of Church and State. Under the *loi Combes* the Radical government of the time indulged in recriminatory policies against Catholics in the public employ, especially in the public schools. There were no laws at the time which effectively protected civil servants against this kind of activity, and it is thus that the Council of State, as supervisor of administrative activity, first came into its own as a protector of individual liberties. It was able to act, of course, only because employees under public contract—civil servants—were involved.

27. A poignant example of such repression, whose importance because of the period should of course not be exaggerated, is recorded in the case of *Chaboury*, Tribunal correctionnel de la Rochelle, November 16,

1939, G.P. 1939. 2. 366:

Whereas the proceedings and testimony show that on October 2, 1939 at about 10 o'clock in the morning Mrs. Lance was present in the tobacconist's shop run by her mother, in the Allé du Mail in La Rochelle, when, speaking of peace to Mr. Chaboury, who was glancing through some newspapers at the door of the shop, he replied to her in these terms: "What difference can it make whether one is French, German, or Russian so long as we have peace?" and then added, "If you could ask those who have fallen whether it would be better to change nationality or die, they would have preferred to change nationality." On hearing these remarks, Miss Chausse, age 24, who was just entering the shop, exclaimed, "Well, not I. I should a hundred times rather die!"—"You, perhaps," retorted Chaboury, "but not everyone."

Whereas the defendant made these remarks on the sidewalk of the public thoroughfare in the presence of two witnesses, and the effect made was such that the police were notified.

Whereas Chaboury first contested the charge by denying the incriminated remarks and then, in the course of the proceedings, admitted having made them, explaining in his defense that he had made them a "friendly" tone, and then as a "joke," an assertion denied by the witnesses;

Whereas these remarks . . . constitute *une information* defined by the decree of September 1, 1939, the word "information" being applicable not only to any announcements or publication of a matter, whether true or not, but also to all remarks made in such conditions as those in which the proud and legitimate indignation of Miss Chausse was aroused.

Whereas in the present circumstances, such remarks are certainly of a nature to exercise a bad influence on the people and the Army . . . Furthermore, their gravity is all the more serious when they come from an individual who is represented in the police report . . . as being a "notorious Communist," It falls to the Court, consequently, to declare (Chaboury) guilty of the offense of which he has been accused and to pronounce an exemplary sentence against him;

For these reasons, declares Chaboury guilty . . . ; sentences him to one year in prison, to ($25) fine and all expenses; orders that the prison sentence be suspended.

28. *The Trial of Emile Zola*, Benjamin R. Tucker, ed., New York, 1898, 355. Ironically, it was the Popular Front Government of Léon Blum that promoted the law transferring press offenses from jury courts to *tribunnaux correctionnels*. This so-called "*Loi Maurras*" of January 10, 1936 was a response to *Action française* propaganda. See Eugene Weber, *Action Française*, Stanford, 1962, 362, 369-70.

184

29. A case in point, Cass. crim. January 31, 1957, *Mouchot*, G.P. 1957, 1, 390: Here the Court of Cassation reversed the Lyons' Court of Appeals' dismissal of charges under the Law of July 16, 1949 against Pierre Mouchot, publisher of children's books, on the grounds that the criminal and immoral acts described in his publications were not presented in a favorable light because their perpetrators were invariably punished, and their heroes "always managed to triumph over their adversaries by means of intelligence, moral strength, generosity, though sometimes, admittedly, by violence, but always used in a good cause." In remanding, the Court of Cassation argued that the lower court had made an "incorrect application" of the law on juvenile publications by failing to see that the mere fact of "happy endings" in children's stories did not necessarily remove from them that character of "flattering young readers' admiration for violence" which it was the purpose of the law to punish.

30. Professor Michel Crozier's description of the position of the prefect within his district reflects a wider realm as well—nothing less, indeed, than attitudes characteristics of modern political system as a whole. See *The Bureaucratic Phenomenon*, Chicago, 1967, 201-2.

> The innovator in a bureaucratic system . . . shows certain special characteristics. He is a legislator, a Solon type, rather than a discoverer. He is someone who will once again put everyone in his own place, who will reorder the world . . . rather than someone who will launch new patterns, new ways of doing things. . . .
>
> Among French bureaucrats, the prefect is probably the one whose innovation-legislation function is most developed. He has discretion and is supposed to use it. Intermediate officials are extremely cautious, timid, and submissive. They pretend that they have no responsibilities whatever in making decisions. They feel that they are merely anonymous helpers of the great innovator figure with whom they identify. Petty officials, on the other hand, appear to be extremely ritualistic and, at the same time, rebellious . . . . They feel themselves betrayed, and their positions undermined, by the prefect's initiative. Their strategy is . . . to impose their ritualism on the prefect and to obtain some compensation for his trespassing on their jobs. . . . This is a protection for the public and . . . for the official as well.

In the perspective offered by this description President de Gaulle was for eleven years the "prefect" of France, surrounded by a self-effacing political and administrative elite who identified with him. The place of the petty officials in Crozier's description is taken in the political system at large by certain classes of other administrators and of the citizens themselves, whose spirit of "rebellion" is given practical expression by the ritualism of which Crozier speaks. Paradoxically, the "innovator's" function is essentially a conservative one, *Bureaucratic Phenomenon*, 235.

31. *J.O.*, *Déb.*, *Ch.*, January 24, 1881, 36. Cf. Irene Collins, *Government and Newspaper Press*, 183-184, citing an editorial in the English *Times* on the occasion of the debates on the Press Law:

> The trust is that when France really has a Press Law it will not be wanted. It is with French journals as with French politicians. Men are demagogues as long as they have to live by their wits. As soon as their circumstances permit, they adopt more moderate opinions. So newspapers without resources try to make a name by scandal and calumny; prosecutions serve to advertise them and they seem to study how to provoke presecutions not serious enough to destroy them. Well-established papers, on the contrary, aim at moderation and avoid legal severity. Several of real weight have passed many years without incurring prosecution, thus showing, not that exceptional legislation makes the Press better but that a better Press makes exceptional laws needless. What France really wants is to escape from the ever-rising flood of newspapers without a mission, conducted by men without culture or conviction, and which can only speculate on exciting unhealthy curiosity. (January 28, 1881).

Notes to Chapter Three

1. Cf. Tocqueville, *The Old Regime and the French Revolution*, Part II, Garden City 1955, *passim*. Also Guy Chapman, *The Third Republic of France, the First Phrase, 1871-1894*, New York, 1963. The regionalization scheme proposed in de Gaulle's referendum of April 1969, whose failure at the polls brought his resignation, does not seem to have been thought by most observers as a fundamental weakening of the centralized administrative system. To have established new regional elected assemblies would, on the contrary, have weakened now established local popular bodies further in the face of a prefectoral system whose administrators owe their power to the central government and its budget, not to local connections.

2. During the nineteenth century, at least until 1881, this role included either buying up opposition newspapers or establishing friendly ones throughout France. See Collins, *Government and Newspaper Press*, Ch. VI, XI, XII, for examples.

3. See, for example, Brian Chapman, *Introduction to French Local Government*, London, 1953, 28-31, and R.K. Gooch, *Regionalism in France*,

New York, 1931, 33-36, who emphasize the close relationship of local government and administrative law. See Articles 91, 97, and 99 of the Law of April 5, 1884 on the mayor's powers. In 1919 the Council of State made clear that the existence of discretionary or police powers of mayors and prefects could not be interpreted to mean that the central government had none: C.E., August 8, 1919, *Labonne*, Rec. 735 (Recueil Lebon, p. 735)

4. See Ch. I above.

5. Cass. crim., March 9, 1914, D. 1919, 1.32.

6. On the legislative declaration of a state of siege see, for example, the law of July 10, 1791, the decree of December 24, 1811, the laws of August 9, 1849 and April 3, 1878, the laws of July 11, 1938, of April 3 and August 7, 1955, March 16, 1956, May 17, 1958 and of course Article 16 of the 1958 Constitution. On the early elaboration of the idea of exceptional circumstances under the Third Republic, see, for example, C.E. August 6, 1915, *Delmotte*, RDP. 1915. 700, concl. Corneille and S. 1916, 3.9, n. Hauriou, and C. E. February 28, 1919, *Dames Dol et Laurent*, S. 1918-1919, 3.33, n. Hauriou.

7. See Jean Jonquères, "Les saisies administratives et judiciaires et la liberté de la presse," G.P. 1967 (1 sem.) doctrine, 35-46.

8. For a description of the day's events and of the circumstances leading up to them, see Max Beloff, "The Sixth of February," in James Joll, ed., *The Decline of the Third Republic*, St. Anthony's Papers No. V, New York, 1959.

9. The *Tribunal des conflits* is made up of an equal number of judges from the Council of State and the Court of Cassation. The Minister of Justice is an ex officio member and may cast the deciding vote in case of equal division.

10. Jonquères, *"Les saisies adminstratives . . ."* 37, notes a decline in use of the *voie de faite* argument since 1955. On the theory of *voie de faite*, which is a wholly customary device, see Georges Védel, "La juridiction compétente pour prévenir, faire cesser, ou réparer la voie de faite", J.C.P. 1950. 1.851, and Long, Weil, Breibant, *Les grands arrêts de le jurisprudence administrative*, Paris, 1962, 211-215.

11. This report of the trial and the quoted materials are drawn from *L'Année Politique*, 1961, Paris, 1962, 25-26, 35.

12. This exchange of letters is reproduced in a later work of Fabreluce's entitled *Le couronnement du Prince*, Paris, 1965.

13. The animal in question was "walrus." But it is an exaggeration to claim that the case against *Haute-Cour* was based solely upon this com-

parison. See the judgment of the *Tribunal correctionnel* reproduced below, pp. 118-122.

14. The practical effect of a restitution of *Haute-Cour* to the publisher prior to the decision of the criminal court would, of course, have been to increase sales enormously. When one considers the fact that no lower court's sentence can be carried out until all possible appeals have been taken, he can imagine that *Haute-Cour* would thus have become a best seller for several years regardless of its (considerable) literary merits.

As for the decision not to sue for damages for the illegal seizure, M. Fabre-Luce's lawyer in the administrative action has written that "our satisfaction has been wholly platonic. We judged that it was preferable not to ask for damages and interest in the light of the fact that these are granted only in case of an inexcusable fault on the part of the Administration: in this instance it would have been difficult to sustain the argument that the Minister of the Interior had committed an inexcusable fault in continuing his seizure of a work that was to be condemned to destruction shortly thereafter." (From a personal letter dated April 25, 1969.) In this particular case justice and utility came to resemble each other strongly, no matter how distinct political theory and legal practice had tried to make them.

15. C. E. June 24, 1960, *Société Frampar et al*, Rec. 412, *concl.* Hermann.

16. See Tribunal civil de la Seine, May 8, 1963 *"Libération" v. Papon, Prefect of Police.* J.C.P. II. 1963, 13894, n. Ch. Debbasch.

17. See Martin Harrison, "Government and Press in France during the Algerian War," *American Political Science Review*, June, 1964, 273-285 for specific examples. Also Yves Galmôt, "Le contrôle jurisdictionnel des saisis d'écrits imprimés", *Etudes et Documents*, Paris, 1959, 57-65, and Long, Weil, Braibant, *Les grands arrêts . . .*, 479-483.

18. See n. 16 above.

19. Cf. J.S. Mill, *On Liberty*, Indianapolis and New York, 1956, 11-12: "In England, from the peculiar circumstances of our political history, though the yoke of opinion is perhaps heavier, that of law is lighter than in most countries of Europe. . . The majority have not yet learned to feel the power of the government their power, and its opinions their opinions. When they do so, individual liberty will probably be as much exposed to invasion from the government as it already is from public opinion."

20. Alfred Grosser, "France: Nothing but Opposition," in Robert A. Dahl, ed., *Political Opposition in Western Democracies*, New Haven, 1966, 284-302.

Notes to Chapter Four

1. Tribunal de Police de Cambrai. December 13, 1961, *de Quental*, G.P. 1961. 1. 21.

2: Cf. Paris Court of Appeals, March 12, 1958, *Pauvert*, RDP. 1958. 141. Here the publisher of a new and elegant edition of Sade's complete works was found guilty of an offense against *bonnes moeurs* under the Law of July 16, 1939 (formerly Article 26 of the Press Law of 1881). Both the trial and the appeals' court found the text in question - *Juliette, ou la prospérité du vice*—pornographic and, indeed, Pauvert admitted as much so far as the general public was concerned. Hence he tried to join issue with a claim that Sade's works were of great importance to certain professions, like medicine, psychiatry, and the social sciences in general, and that publication of the complete works was a service to them, since clinicians and scholars would no longer have to depend on commentaries and glosses of uncertain merit. Both courts found Pauvert's intent to be at odds with his professed purposes. The trial court declared in particular:

> Contrary to [Pauvert's] assertions, the facts that this edition was offered by subscription and printed in limited numbers are not sufficient to establish [absence of guilty intent . . . especially as] he arranged to advertise the work in *Le Crapouillot*, a periodical which cannot be considered as a publication with a particularly scientific, psychological, or medical orientation. And it is not without significance that this advertisement appears . . . on the same page with a list of other erotic books . . . In any case, Pauvert admits to having sent out subscription bulletins for his edition . . . in which he calls "daring" even those texts which are not, and in which he announces that although "some of Sade's works are normally publishable because they do not include . . . any legally reprehensible rawness of expression, the daring works are reserved for a private edition that only a small number can acquire." Hence, contrary to his claim, the ultimate purpose, even if it were established, must not be confused with the guilty intent, [which] is constituted by his knowledge of the outrageous character . . . of the work whose publication he undertook.

The practical difference between the trial and appeals courts' judgments came to this: the appeals court reduced the $160 fine imposed by the trial court to $50, suspended sentence, and ordered the seized copies deposited in state libraries under a provision of law that commands works of an "artistic, literary, historical, or philosophical character" to be preserved rather than destroyed. In French parlance, Pauvert's edition was thereby consigned to "Hell."

3. Tribunal correctionnel d'Orange, April 19, 1950, *Nigoul et al*, G.P. 1950. 2. 35.

4. Bourges, August 17, 1877, *Th* . . . , S. 1877. 2. 297. In the same vein, see Tribunal correctionnel de la Seine, December 18, 1946, *Baudet v. Cachin et le Journal l'Humanité*, G.P. 1946 2. 133. There, the court held that the phrase "M. Baudet . . . can develop in complete liberty the fascist program for colonial enslavement" contained an allegation injurious to the honor and esteem of Baudet, "all the more regrettable," said the court, because the plaintiff had supplied evidence showing his adherence to the Resistance movement from its very beginning. Cf. Cour d'appel de Chambéry, October 22, 1936, *Roche v. Bozon-Vielle*, G. P. 1936. 2 780., in which the judges distinguished between the "objective" and defamatory uses of the word "fascist." Also Tribunal corr. de Perigueux, November 22, 1929, G.P. 1930. 35, where the epithet in question was "Communist."

5. Tribunal correctionnel de la Seine, December 7, 1945, *Frenay v. le Journal l'Humanité*, G. P. 1946. 1. 81.

6. Tribunal civil de la Seine. November 20, 1957. *Confédération Nationale de la boulangerie et al* v. *Société d' Edition et de Publications du Journal "La Presse" et le Sieur d'Almeida.* G.P. 1958, 1. 94. Ct. Cour d'appel de Paris, June 16, 1960, *Confédération Nationale des industries et commerces en gros des vins, sirops, spiritueux et liqueurs de France* v. *Navarro, Editions Lug et le Comité National de défense contre l'alcoolisme*, G. P. 1960, 2. 158. In this case the court found that a journalist's attack on the "enticing publicity" of *apéritifs* not only was not defamatory but highly praiseworthy in light of the "well-known curse of alcoholism in France today."

7. Article 1382 of the Civil Code—"Any act whatever by which one person causes injury to another, obliges him by whom the injury has been caused to make reparation for it"—is the legal basis for civil suits in libel and slander. Actions for civil damages can obviously be as threatening to freedom of the press as criminal suits, especially as in France the traditional awards of damages in the latter case is one franc. The customary use of the criminal law as an instrument of repression in matters of defamation in France reflects well the "tutellary" view of the state that was held by the Opportunists in 1881. Prior to the *Ordonnance* of May 6, 1944, the defense of truth was very strictly limited to political and financial affairs. As in eighteenth century English law, defamations stating the truth were considered as disruptive of the good order of society as those based on falsehoods. The 1944 reform made available the defense of truth is a wider range of cases, the purpose being to reduce the number of defamation suits undertaken. In the eyes of those who regard a sort of conventional moral order in society as vital, litigiousness itself is not the least threat, and the older rule seemed to encourage suits on the part of those who were safe from having to show counterproof of truth.

8. For one view of what happened at Pont-Saint-Esprit, see John G. Fuller. *The Day of St. Anthony's Fire.* New York, 1968.

9. Article 226 of the Penal Code: Whosoever will have publicly sought to throw discredit on a judicial act or decision, whether by acts, speeches, or writings, in conditions such as to bring harm to the authority of justice or its independence, will be punished by from one to six months in prison and from ($100 to $5,000) fine, or one of these punishments only. The court may order that its judgment will be placarded and published as it chooses, at the expense of the condemned, so long as this expense is no greater than the maximum of the fine provided for above. The preceding provisions may in no case be applied to purely technical commentaries, nor to acts, words or writings aimed at bringing about a review of the verdict. . . .

10. The text of this and the following materials are drawn from the court reports. See Tribunal correctionnel de Montbeliard, June 28, 1963, *Schroedt*, G. P. 1963. 2. 350. For a similar judgment, on appeal to the Court of Cassation, see Cass. crim. February 11, 1965, *Lazareff and Grandmougin*, J. C. P. 1965. II 14128 *bis.*

11. Tribunal de grande instance de la Seine, 17 e chambre correctionnelle, October 9, 1965, *Ministre public v. Laurent et al*, as reported in Jacques Laurent, *Offenses au Chef de l'Etat*, Paris, 1965, 227-8.

12. Tribunal de grande instance de la Seine, 17e chambre correctionnelle, December 20, 1963, *Ministre public v. Veuve Julliard et Fabre-Luce.* Because the text of this judgment was ordered not to be published, I am indebted to counsel for Monsieur Fabre-Lauce for it.

13. Commentaries, as cited in Marvin Summers, *Free Speech and Political Protest*, Boston, 1967, vii.

14. Roger Pinto, *La liberté d'opinion et d'information; contrôle jurisdictionel et contrôle administratif*, Paris, 1955, 50, n. 127.

15. See n. 10, p. 90 above.

16. *Revolutionary Syndicalism in France*, Cambridge, England, 1970, 23.

17. Cass. crim. February 6, 1907, *Griffuehles et autres*, Bul. n. 52. For other cases illustrating uses of Article 25 of the Press Law see Cass. crim. February 26, 1926, *Guilbert*, G. P. 1926. 1. 584; Cour d'appel de Paris, March 27, 1935, *Frayon*, G. P. 1935. 2. 5; The particular concern in both the cases cited here was the attempt to assess the delictuous writings as "anarchistic" in content, in order that the defendants might be tried before *tribunaux correctionnels*, with their more summary procedures, rather than before assize courts, where a jury trial was necessary. The first exception to the latter's jurisdiction for free speech cases

came in 1893 with passage of the so-called *lois scélérates*, which were aimed at repressing anarchist attacks. Other exceptions were made by the Popular Front Government with a view to repressing particularly Maurras' attacks more expeditiously.

For cases illustrating uses of Article 84 of the Penal Code, which punishes "knowing participation in an enterprise to demoralize the army for the purpose of weakening national security" see Cour d'appel de Nancy, October 10, 1950, *Finkelstein*, G. P. 1951. 1. 151; G. P. 1951. 1.21; Tribunal corr. de Beauvais, December 20, 1950, *Janeau et Vigne*, G. P. 1951, 1. 200. Also Cass. crim. May 2, 1956, *Merot*, Bul. no. 38 and Bul no. 339. No doubt one of the broadest statutory attempts to limit speech was contained in the Law of July 31, 1920, today substantially abrogated, that prohibited any propaganda in favor of family planning or birth control, or dissemination of any information about contraception. See Cass. crim. February 20, 1937, *Dame Humbert*, G. P. 1939. 1.953. Pinto, *La liberté d'opinion* . . . , 88-9.

18. Cass. crim. August 22, 1912, Bul. no 464.

19. Cass. crim. February 11, 1954, *Bardèche*, G. P. 1954 1.131. Cf. Cour d'appel de Paris, February 25, 1959, *Malliavin*, D. 1959. 1.552. Editor of the rightist weekly *Rivarol*, Malliavin was successfully prosecuted for criticizing an issue of postage stamps in 1958 commemorating certain "heroes of the Resistance," in aid of General de Gaulle's then somewhat shaky claims to legitimacy. Malliavin charged that the stamps were unjustly partial to the Resistance movement, and that they constituted what he called "Totalitarian Philately." He urged that a similar set of stamps be issued in favor of those whom he called "heroes of the collaboration." He was condemned on the grounds that his recommendation constituted an apology for the crimes committed by the collaborationists.

20. Cass. crim. October 29, 1936. *Maurras and Deleste*, G. P. 1936. 2. 684.

21. *The Old Regime and the French Revolution*, Gilbert Stuart tr., Garden City, 1955, 167.

Notes to Chapter Five

1. From a radio debate with Valéry Giscard d'Estaing on Radio Luxembourg, September 2, 1968. See also his *La révolution introuvable*, Paris, 1968.

2. *The Old Regime and the French Revolution*. Gilbert, tr., Garden City, 1955, 210-211.

3. *Ibid.*

4. See, for example, A. J. Beitzinger, *A History of American Political Thought*, New York and Toronto, 1972: esp. pp. 232-242. "An American Science of Politics and Law."

5. Tocqueville, *Democracy in America*, xiii-xv.

6. *The First and Second Discourses*. Roged Masters, ed., New York, 1964, 51.

7. *The Social Contract*, I.

8. Rousseau's work again characteristically reflects the search for identity. In Emile, for example, the tutor plays a role equivalent to that of the general will as legislator for the body politic, allowing the boy, through carefully prepared experiences, to "discover" those relationships with the moral and empirical worlds that will serve him in the vicissitudes of life. The author thus doubts whether the mind can be self-creating; certainly, for him, not the mind of a child. As to the mind of society creating itself, Rousseau again supposes the intervention of a godlike legislator to be required.
It is the transcendental openendedness of this divine connection which gives ultimate meaning to the whole political enterprise, since no a-historical logic can in his view be self-justifying.

9. Cf. Hans Barth, *The Idea of Order*, Dordrecht, 1960, 6, 173-175, 196. Also Dorothy Lee, *Freedom and Culture*, Englewood Cliffs, 1959, 72-75.

10. See Montaigne's *Essays*, "The Apology for Raymond Sébond."

11. Cf. Angustine. *City of God*, XIX, 6, Garden City, 1958, 444.

12. Montesquieu, *Persian Letters*, Loy, tr., New York, 1961, 166. Letter LXXXIII.

13. *On Liberty*, New York, 1947, 10.

14. Mill tries to escape this dilemma by arguing that though God is omniscient. He cannot be omnicompetent. It is thus up to men to complete the work the divine hand has bungled, once they can grasp the divine plan. See his three posthumous essays, esp. "Nature."

15. Laurence Wylie in Stanley Hoffman et al, *In Search of France*, Cambridge, Mass., 1963, 204.

16. Jacques Maritain, *Man and the State*, Chicago, 1961, 10-11.

17. *Philosophical Dictionary*, "Liberty of the Press."

18. *Discourse on the Arts and Sciences*, Roger D. Masters, ed., *The First and Second Discourses*, New York, 1964, 50.

19. Paul Cambon, *Correspondance*, 1870-1924, Vol. I, Paris 1945, 355. Cited in Guy Chapman, *The Dreyfus Case*, London, 1955, 12.

20. See, for example. A.T. Von Mehren, *The Civil Law System*, Englewood Cliffs, 1957, ch. 8.

21. On the sense of immediate public necessity as one of the "general principles of the law" recognized in the jurisprudence of the Council of State see my "Constitutionalism and the Judiciary in France," LXXX *PSQ* 1, 80-83 especially. Cf. Paul A. Freund, *The Supreme Court*, Cleveland, 1961, 33; speaking of the "hierarchy of values" implicit in the Court's decisions in recent civil liberties cases interpreting the due process clause of the 14th Amendment, a clause with some of the same potential as the "general principles of the law."

22. Tocqueville, *The Old Regime and the French Revolution*, Stuart tr., Garden City, 1955, xiii.

23. See Laurence Wylie, "Change at the Grass Roots," in Stanley Hoffman and others, *In Search of France*, Cambridge (Mass.) 1963, 227: "Symbolic expression in France . . . is more elaborately and subtly developed than in most cultures. . . ." Cf. Harvey Waterman, *Political Change* in France, Columbus, 1969, 113-142 *passim*. "We have seen a continued penchant for abstraction on the part of the intellectuals, but (also) the possibility of some shift from the philosophical kind to the scientific kind--that is, a secularization of politics."128. Yet "the expectation that politics must be subsumed under ethical and metaphysical principles remains, and may well be one source of the important political success of Charles de Gaulle."120.

24. From E. Barker, *Social Contract*, London, 1960, 249. Bk. III. ix.

Bibliography

H. B. Acton. "The Philosophy of Language in Revolutionary France," in J. N. Findlay, *Studies in Philosophy,* London, 1966.

Irène Allier, "Ces messieurs de la Cour," *Esprit,* 1954.

F. M. Anderson, "*The Constitutions and Other Select Document Illustrative of the History of France, 1789-1907,* Minneapolis, 1908.

F.A. Allen, *The Borderland of Criminal Justice, Essays in Law and Criminology,* Chicago, 1964.

Jacques Barzun, *On Human Freedom,* Boston, 1939.

H. Arnault de Guényveau. *Discours prononcé par Monsieur Arnault de Guenyveau à la rentrée de la Cour d'appel de Rennes, le 16 ocobre 1890,* Rennes, 1890.

Hans Barth, *The Idea of Order, Contributions to a Philosophy of Politics,* Hankamer and Newell, tr., Dordrecht, 1960.

Eugène Blum, *La Déclaration des droits de l'homme et du citoyen,* Paris, 1902.

Jean Bodin, *Six Books of the Commonwealth,* M. J. Tooley, tr. and abrg., n. d., London.

William Bosworth, *Catholicism and Crisis in Modern France,* Princeton, 1963.

William J. Brennan, Jr., "The Supreme Court and the Meiklejohn Interpretation of the First Amendment," 79 *Harvard Law Review* 1 (1965).

Richard Brandt, ed., *Social Justice,* Englewood Cliffs, 1962.

Léon Brunschvicg, *Descartes et Pascal, lecteurs de Montaigne,* Paris 1944.

Sybille Bedford, *The Faces of Justice, a Traveller's Report,* New York, 1961.

P. J. Belton, "The Control of Group Defamation: a Comparative Study of Law and Its Limitations," *Tulane Law Review* 34 (1960), Paris, 1956.

André Besson, *Cours de droit penal.*

T. Bouffandeau, "La délimination de la compétence de la juridiction administrative par la jurisprudence du Tribunal des conflits," *Le Conseil d'Etat, Livre Jubilaire,* 1952. Jean Boulanger, "Principles généraux du droit et droit positif, "*Mélanges Ripert,* T. 1. Paris, 1955.

André Bruzin et Jean Nectoux, *Jurisprudence française,* 1807-a 1952; periode 1807-1926; *grands arrêts de principe:* période 1927-1952; *toutes décisions notables publiées dans le Jurisclasseur Périodique (Semaine Juridique) et dans d'autres recueils généraux,* Paris, 1954.

Georges Burdeau. *Les libertés publiques,* 2nd ed., Paris, 1961.

Benjamin Cardozo, *The Nature of the Judicial Process.* New Haven, 1921.

Frede Castberg. *Freedom of Speech in the West,* New York and Oslo, 1960.

Edmund Cahn, ed., *The Great Rights,* New York, 1963.

_____. "*The Consumers of Injustice,*" *XXVI Social Research* 2 (1959).

Huntington Cairns, *Law and Its Premises*, New York, 1962.

Casamayor, *Les juges,* Paris, 1957.

René Cassin, "Le Conseil d'Etat, gardien des principes de la Révolution française, "*Revue Internationale d'histoire politique et constituitionnelle,* Brussles, January-February, 1951.

Brian Chapman, "The French Conseil d'Etat," XII *Parliamentary Affairs* 2, (1959).

_____, *Introduction to French Local Government*, London, 1953.

Henri Chardon, "Etudes sur l'organization de la République," *Revue politique et littéraire (Revue bleue),* Paris, 1917.

D. G. Charlton, *Positivist Thought in France during the Second Empire, 1852-1870*, London, 1959.

_____, *Secular Religions of France, 1815-1870*, London, 1963.

Raymond Charles, *La justice en France,* Paris, 1958.

R. E. Charlier, *Cours de droit public,* Paris, 1957.

J.-J. Chevallier, *Cours de droit public,* Paris, 1959.

W. F. Church, *Constitutional Thought in Sixteenth Century France, a Study in the Evolution of Ideas,* Cambridge, Mass., 1941.

Morris R. Cohen, "The Place of Logic in the Law," in Harvard Law Review, *An Introduction to Law,* Cambridge, 1957.

C. A. Colliard, *Les libertés publiques,* Paris, 1958.

Irene Collins, *The Government and the Newspaper Press in France,* 1814-1881, London, 1959.

J.-L. Costa, "Nécessité, conditions et limites d'un pouvoir judiciaire en France," *Revue française de science politique,* June, 1960.

L. G. Crocker, *An Age of Crisis: Man and World in 18th Century French Thought,* Baltimore, 1959.

Pierre Dareste, *Les voies de recours contre les actes de la puissance publique,* Paris, 1914.

René David and Henry de Vries, *The French Legal System: an Introduction to Civil Law Systems,* New York, 1958.

H. A. Deane, *The Political and Social Ideas of St. Augustine,* New York, 1963.

G. Davras, "La liberté d'expression et le décret du 29 juillet 1939." *Etudes de presse,* No. 8, Paris, 1947.

John Dewey, *My Philosophy of Law,* Boston, 1941.

Patrick Devlin. *The Enforcement of Morals,* London, 1959.

Louis Ducloux, *From Blackmail to Treason, Political Crime and Corruption in France, 1920-1940,* Matthews, tr., London, 1958.

Léon Duguit, *Le droit social, le droit individuel et la transformation de l'état,* Paris, 1922.

Emile Durkheim, *Professional Ethics and Civic Morals,* Glencoe, 195.

D. M. Eastwood, *The Revival of Pascal: a Study of His Relation to Modern French Thought,* London, 1936.

Mario Einaudi, *The Physiocratic Doctrine of Judicial Control,* Cambridge, Mass., 1938.

A. P. d'Entrèves, *Natural Law, an Introduction to Legal Philos-*

ophy, London, 1963.

T. I. Emerson, "Toward a General Theory of the First Amendment," 72 *Yale Law Journal* 5, (1963).

Alfred Fabre-Luce, *Le couronnement du Prince*, Paris, 1965.

Albert Feuillerat, *French Life and Ideals*, New Haven, 1925.

Felix Frankfurter, *Law and Politics*, New York, 1962.

C. E. Freedeman, *The Conseil d'Etat in Modern France*, New York, 1961.

Paul A. Freund, *The Supreme Court of the United States, Its Business, Purposes and Performance*, Cleveland, 1961.

_____, "Social Justice and the Law," in Richard Brandt, ed., *Social Justice*, Englewood Cliffs, 1962.

Lon Fuller, *The Law in Search of Itself*, Chicago, 1940.

_____, *The Morality of the Law*, New Haven, 1964.

W. B. Gallie, *Philosophy and the Historical Understanding*, New York, 1961.

Yves Galmôt, "Le contrôle juridictionnel des saisies d'ecrits imprimés," *Etudes et Documents* (Conseil d'Etat), Paris, 1959.

Maurice Garçon, *Défense de la liberté individuelle*, Paris, 1957.

_____, *Histoire de la Justice sous la IIIè Republique*, Paris, 1957.

B. D. Graham, "Theories of the French Party System under the Third Republic," *XII Political Studies* 1, (1964).

Andre Gidé, *Souvenirs de la cour d'assises*, Paris, 1924.

Morris Ginsberg, "The Concept of Justice," *Plilosophy*, April, 1963.

R. K. Gooch, *Regionalism in France*, New York, 1931.

Raymond Guillien, "Les commissaires du gouvernement . . . près le Conseil d'Etat," *Revue du droit public*, 1955.

Henry M. Hart, Jr., "Holmes' Positivism—an Addendum," *An Introduction to Law*, Cambridge, Mass., 1957.

Eugène Hatin, *Manuel théorioue et pratique de la liberté de la presse*, Paris, 1868.

Daniel Halévy, *La fin des notables*, Paris, 1937.

H. L. A. Hart, *The Concept of Law,* London, 1961.

_____, *Law, Liberty, and Morality*, London, 1963.

_____, *The Morality of the Criminal Law*, Jerusalem, 1965.

C. J. Hamson, *Executive Discretion and Judicial Control, an Aspect of the French Conseil d'Etat*, London, 1954.

Pierre Hébraux, "Justice '59-," *Recueil Dalloz, Chroniques*, 1959.

W. E. Hocking, *Freedom of the Press, a Framework of Principle*, Chicago,, 1947.

O. W. Holmes, Jr., *The Common Law*, Cambridge, Mass., 1963.

——————, *Collected Legal Papers*, New York, 1920.

——————, *Holmes-Laski Correspondence*, Hiss, ed., and abrg., Princeton, 195.

S. P. Huntington, "Political Modernization: Europe v. America," *World Politics* (1966).

Jean Jonquères, "Les saisies administratives et judiciaires et la liberté de la presse," *Gazette du Palais*, 1er sem., 1967.

Jacques Kayser, *La mort d'une liberté*, Paris, 1955.

A. de Laubadère, *Les libertés publiques*, Paris, 1955.

——————, *Manuel de droit administratif*, Paris, 1960.

Louis Lachance, *Le droit moderne et les droits de l'homme*, Paris, 1959.

M. Letourneur et J. Méric, *Conseil d'Etat et juridictions administratives*, Paris, 1955.

Jacques Laurent, *Offenses au Chef de l'Etat*, Paris, 1965.

J.–C. Laurent, "La correctionnalisation." *Juris-Classeur Périodique*, 1950, 1.

Edward H. Levi, *An Introduction to Legal Reasoning*, Chicago, 1949.

Raymond Manévy, *La presse de la IIIe République*, Paris, 1955.

Jacques Maritain, *Man and the State*, Chicago, 1951.

——————, *The Range of Reason*, London, 1953.

Yvonne Marx, "Le mouvement de 'la défense sociale'," *Esprit*, 1954.

Charles H. McIlwain, *Constitutionalism: Ancient and Modern*, rev. ed., Ithaca, 1947.

Wallace Mendelson, "On the Meaning of the First Amendment: Absolutes in the Balance," 50 *California Law Review* (1962).

Perry Miller, *The Legal Mind in America from Independence to the Civil War*, Garden City, 1962.

Henri Motulsky, "L'état actuel de la philosophie et de la science du Droit en France," *Etudes de droit contemporain*, Paris, 1957.

A. Morange, "Valeur juridique des principes contenues dans les déclarations de droits," *Revue du droit public*, 1945.

G. O. W. Mueller, ed., and Jean F. Moreau, tr., *The French Penal Code*, New York, 1960.

Le club Jean Moulin, *L'Etat et le citoyen*, Paris, 1961.

F. S. C. Northrop, *The Complexity of Legal and Ethical Experience*, Boston, 1959.

Francis Oakley, "Medieval Theories of Natural Law: William of Occam and the Significance of the Voluntarist Tradition," VI *Natural Law Forum* (1961).

Alexander Pekelis, *Law and Social Action*, Ithaca, 1950.

Roger Pinto, *Le liberté d'opinion et d'information; contrôle juridictionnel et contrôle administratif*, Paris, 1955.

M. Patin, "La répression des délits de presse," *Revue de science criminelle*, 1954.

Roscoe Pound, *The Spirit of the Common Law*, Boston, 1921.

_____, "Common Law and Legislation," *An Introduction to Law*, Cambridge, Mass., 1957.

Jean Rivéro, "Le juge administratif français: un juge qui gouverne?" *Dalloz Hébdomadaire, Chronique*, February 8, 1951.

Arnold M. Rose, "Voluntary Associations in France," in Rose, ed., *Theory and Method in the Social Sciences*, Minneapolis, 1954.

Eugene Rostow, "The Democratic Nature of Judicial Review," 66 *Harvard Law Review* 2.

Bernard Schwartz, ed., *The Code Napoleon and the Common-Law World*, New York, 1956.

Herbert J. Spiro, *Government by Constitution*, New York, 1959.

Pierre Souty, *Recueil de jurisprudence en matière constitutionnelle et de libertés publiques*, Paris, 1950.

James F. Stephens, *Liberty, Equality, and Fraternity*, London, 1873.

Julius Stone, *The Province and Function of Law*, Cambridge,

Mass., 1950.

David Thomson, *Democracy in France*, 2nd. ed., London, 1952.

Samuel M. Thompson, "The Authority of Law," LXXV *Ethics* 1, 1964.

Ernst Troeltsch, "The Ideas of Natural Law and Humanity in World Politics," in E. Barker, ed., of Otto Gierke, *Natural Law and the Theory of Society, 1500-1800*, Boston, 1957.

Koang-Mou Tchou, *La saisie des journaux et imprimés*, (thesis) Paris, 1937.

Armin Uhler, *Review of Administrative Acts*, Chicago, 1942.

Geroge Védel, "L'inexpériencc constitutionnelle de la France," *La Nef, nouvelles séries*, April-June, 1961.

A. T. von Mehren, *The Civil Law System, Cases and Materials for the Comparative Study of Law*, Englewood Cliffs, 1957.

Harvey Waterman, *Political Change in Comtemporary France, the Politics of an Industrial Democracy*, Columbus, 1969.

Laurence Wylie, *Village in the Vaucluse*, rev. ed., New York, 1964.

—————, "Social Change at the Grass Roots," in Hoffmann and others, *In Search of France*, Cambridge, Mass., 1963.

M. Wohlgemouth, *Des droits individuels et de leur garantie judiciaire spécialement contre le pouvoir législatif,* Paris, 1906.

Collections

Recueil Dalloz (D, DH, or DP.)

Recueil Sirey (S)

Gazette de Palais (G. P.)

Juris-Classeur Périodique (La Semaine Juridique) (J. C.P.)

Revue du Droit Public (RDP)

Code Pénal, annoté d'après la doctrine et la jurisprudence, Dalloz, 1962.

Rivière, Hélie, Pont, *Codes Français et Lois usuelles*, Paris, 1889.

Index

Index of Excerpted Cases